Diverse Dialogues

A COLLECTION OF 10 MINUTE PLAYS

By Carolyn Hughes-Bronson and Judith Weston

Diverse Dialogues
A Collection of 10 Minute Plays
©2023, Carolyn Hughes-Bronson & Judith Weston

Although the play "The Letter" is based on a historical event the characters portrayed are fictitious. In this collection of 10-minute plays, any resemblances and composites of events are purely coincidental to persons both living and deceased.

ISBN: 979-8-35092-693-4
ISBN eBook: 979-8-35092-694-1

TABLE OF CONTENTS

GRANDMA'S SECRET

Two granddaughters reminiscing about their grandmother, discover her trunk, and eventually her secret.

CHARACTERS

African American female-Bev- age 30+

African American female-Roz - age 30+

African American male-Mr. McFarland/Grandpa - age 80+

African American female-Ms. Willard age - 70+

STAGE SETTING

On the far right of the stage, there is a bed and a sitting chair. Lying on the bed is a robe, and a pair of pink house slippers are on the floor. Behind the bed hidden by an old quilt is a medium-sized chest. There is a cane for grandpa to help him walk.

The stage on the right is dark where the bed is located, the left side is illuminated and in walk the four actors.

MS. WILLARD

Well . . . I better be getting on now but, Mr. McFarland, Bev, Roz . . . I sure am sorry for your loss, our choir is not going to sound the same. Betty always brought us to tears singing the way she did . . . her rendition of "The Old Rugged Cross" always brought me to *my* knees, and believe me, these knees have seen some bending! She sure was a precious soul. Oh (she reaches toward Mr. McFarland and touches his arm), by the way, I cooked up some greens and cornbread; they're on your kitchen counter.

GRANDPA

Thank you, Ms. Willard, we appreciate that. (Bev and Roz nod.)

MS. WILLARD

Please let me know if I can do anything, I'm here for you all . . . (she slowly shakes her head) . . . sure going to miss her. . . . Well, I'll keep you all in my prayers, goodbye. (She shakes their hands and leaves.)

BEV

Grandpa, why don't you go rest in the den? Roz and I will start packing your things; we've all been through a lot these past few days . . . but I'm glad you have decided to live with Uncle Leonard. He and you were always close until he had to move to New Jersey. When I talked to him the other day, he said he's glad that he's going to finally get a chance to beat you at checkers! (Grandpa laughs.)

GRANDPA

In his dreams! (They share a laugh.) Ok, I got an easy chair with my name on it, and listen, don't you two be going into your grandma's room. *I'll* see about that tomorrow.

BEV, ROZ

Ok, Grandpa. (They look at each other and shrug.)

(Grandpa exits stage using his cane.)

BEV

Ohhh, this is harder than I thought. (She looks around and grows melancholy.) What are we going to do with all these things that hold so much meaning? I don't know how or where to start.

ROZ

I know, Bev. (She takes her sister's hand.) I . . . oh . . . just when I thought I wasn't going to cry anymore. (She starts to sob.)

BEV

Ok . . . it's ok. (She says sympathetically, then takes a deep breath and exhales and a smile begins to grow on her face.)

Hey, Roz . . . do you remember the corner in the living room? Grammy called it our "special place." After we were all cleaned up from playing, she'd have us put our pj's on and . . .

ROZ

She'd sit us down with our bedtime snack of milk and one cookie (she holds up one finger) and she'd dim the lights . . .

BEV

And then she'd tell us stories from the olden days of playing hopscotch, marbles, and chasing fireflies. (She says with a wistful smile.) And remember the story of the stars?

ROZ

How could I forget? She'd hug us together and say what she would always say... (Using a voice that resembles her grandma) "You know what those stars are *really* doing up there in that big old sky? You see them twinkling . . . they're really winking. That's our Lord Jesus letting us know that He is watching over us while we sleep, and He will keep us in His care . . . even in the dark . . . because His light is always on." Then she would wink at us both. (They both laugh and start to look around.)

BEV

I know Grandpa said don't go into her room, but . . . I . . . don't think he'd mind really . . . just to peek in. I . . . really . . .

ROZ

Ok . . . I really want to, too.

(Bev and Roz now walk toward the bed; the light fades where they were and now the bed area is illuminated. They hold hands and then sit on the bed.)

ROZ

Oh, it's Grammy's robe. (She picks it up and hugs it close to her and inhales deeply.) Chanel number 5; I just loved watching her spray it on from that vintage perfume bottle, while getting ready for church.

BEV

Speaking of church, remember sitting behind Sister Perry? Now there's a lady that could've used a spritz of Chanel number 5. (They laugh.)

ROZ

Girl, if Grammy was here, she'd wash both of our mouths out with soap. (They laugh.)

BEV

That's true . . . (she sighs). So many things I wanted to say to her . . . (she stands up and looks around, then notices something behind the bed.)

Hey . . . I wonder what this is.

ROZ

Bev . . . Grandpa said—

BEV

I know . . . but I just . . . really quick .... take a look, then we'll leave. (She lifts the quilt, then sees the trunk.)

Oh! What's *this*?

(She pulls it around to the edge of the bed where Roz is now sitting.)

ROZ

Go ahead . . . let's just take a quick peek and then leave.

(Bev opens the trunk, and both their eyes get big. Bev begins to reach in and holds up large pasties to her chest.)

BEV

GRANDMA . . . was . . . a . . .

BEV AND ROZ

STRIPPER???

GRANDPA

(Re-enters the room and clears his throat loudly)

Burlesque dancer . . . that's an entertainer!

BEV AND ROZ

(Both look toward him shocked.) *GRANDPA!*

GRANDPA

(He laughs and shakes his head) Now didn't I tell you two not to go in your grandma's room?

(He starts to smile and walks toward them, his cane clacking on the floor toward the pair and sits in the chair.) I should've known you two girls would not mind your old grandpa! Well . . . go ahead; you opened that chest . . . no sense in closing it now.

(He smiles broadly, and the girls continue to pull items from the chest: sheer scarves, full length gloves, revealing gown, pasties, short skirts with fringe, mesh stockings, and a hat with large feathers.)

GRANDPA

Yes . . . it was at . . . (he laughs) Black Eden; that's what folks called a little place in Michigan, Black Eden . . . Idlewild, Michigan, where everyone felt like family . . . a place to escape the unpleasantries of the time.

BEV

What?

(Roz has her eyes on the items being pulled from the chest; they have been placing them on the bed.)

GRANDPA

Yes . . . that's right, Idlewild. It all started around 1912 and began to flourish; it was a place where every door was open no matter the color of your skin. Whites and Blacks intermingled easily, casually. Do you know that you could have a conversation with W. E. B. Du Bois one moment then have cocktails with Madame C.J. Walker, who made over a million dollars selling her beauty products, the next!

But it wasn't all for the intellectual gatherings. It was the *entertainment* . . . You could see Cab Calloway or Etta James, B.B. King, and Sarah Vaughn to name a few.

ROZ

Grandpa! *Why* didn't you or Grandma tell us? That sounds like an amazing story!

GRANDPA

Well, for one thing, your mom before she passed, made your grandmother and me promise to make the right decision when it came time to talk about the past, so now (He smiles lovingly) you two snoopers have forced my hand! (He laughs.) Your grandma just never got around to it . . . kept putting it off. Oh . . . I guess it's time to tell you how I *met* your grandma.

BEV

Wasn't it at the Five and Dime?

GRANDPA

Well . . . no. . . . (He shakes his head and smiles.) Here's the real story.

ROZ

Grandpa!

GRANDPA

I know. (He laughs.) Well . . . one night, while I was tending bar at the Paradise Club—that's one of the clubs in Idlewild—the announcer who had taken the stage came out and got our attention, then he spoke in the microphone. "Ladies and Gentlemen! Tonight . . . we have something very special for you . . . in her one-night-only appearance. . . .. The one you've all heard about . . . the lady that can shimmy and shift her silky self in every direction! Would you please give a warm welcome to our very own . . . the one. . . the only . . . Mocha Mae North, South, East and . . . West!

BEV AND ROZ

Wow!

ROZ

That's one heck of a stage name.

GRANDPA

Well, she earned it.

I saw her shimmy as she parted through the velvet curtains dressed in a long flowing red dress, and matching gloves; her hair was all pinned up with silver tassels that twinkled like stars that fell around her neck . . .

BEV

Oh, Grandpa, that's so *sweet* sounding!

GRANPA

Well . . . Roz, Bev, your old grandpa *did* dabble in poetry . . . especially during that time . . .

BEV

You *never* told us about that either!

GRANDPA

(He laughs.) There's a lot I haven't told you obviously! (He laughs again.) Anyway . . . as I was saying . . . well . . . I asked my buddy Charlie to cover for me and then I walked casually toward the stage door where the dancers would exit.

The door was partially lit and out she came walking down the stairs and . . . (he pauses as if in mid-thought) I don't know if fate intervened on my behalf or what, but she *stumbled* . . .right into my arms....and at that moment I thought I had died . . . because in my arms . . . (he holds out his arms as if holding someone) right there on those steps, I was holding a piece of heaven . . .

(Roz and Bev are dabbing their eyes while he reaches for his handkerchief that's in his pocket and dabs his eyes). She looked at me and I at her, and that was it.

ROZ

Oh, Grandpa!

BEV

So sweeeeeet!

GRANDPA

I know. . .. (He looks down for a moment then speaks.) Hey . . . let's go on down to the kitchen . . . we got Ms. Willard's greens and cornbread with our names on it! All this talking is making me hungry! (He smiles.)

BEV

What do you want us to do with Grandma's things?

GRANDPA

Well, let's you, me, and Roz talk about that in the kitchen . . . and Roz . . . can you whip up some of your famous sweet tea?

ROZ

Oh, Grandpa..you know I will... that's my special (She winks) ...tea!

(Grandpa and Roz start walking and have almost disappeared off stage, and while they aren't looking, Bev grabs the hat and scarf and puts them on; she looks up for a moment, smiles broadly, then starts her own shimmying around, then turns after them laughing.)

Lights out.

THE END

THE LIFE COACH

A woman laments about her body issues to avoid talking about what's really bothering her.

CHARACTERS

Female-Ruth - age 60+

Female-Denise - age 50+

STAGE SETTING

Two chairs

One full-length mirror

One full-length lamp

Ruth is dressed in an old motorcycle t-shirt with cutoff sleeves, a bandana around her head, blue jeans and boots. Denise has hair pinned up and is smartly dressed in professional attire.

DENISE

I'm so glad you've decided to come in. You've backed out several times, and I do understand, but as your coach, I have already assessed you as being someone who is afraid and is quite skeptical. Am I correct? Oh, by the way, is that a Rebel you rode up on?

RUTH

Well, I wouldn't say afraid, I kept canceling because I couldn't pay your fee, and yeah ... it's a Rebel ... rides nice too.

DENISE

I see, honesty . . . honesty is a solid attribute necessary to move forward; it keeps unnecessary baggage from weighing us down.

RUTH

It's pretty hard to ditch my baggage . . . I've been carrying most of it since '72, especially this one.

(Ruth gets up and smacks her behind.)

Well, I'm here really because I figured if my heart was having problems, I certainly would go see a heart doctor and if I was having difficulty breathing, I would definitely see a lung doctor . . . so . . . I'm losing at life. So here I am, and my friends thought it would be a good thing . . .,

(Ruth pauses and looks over at Denise) *coach*.

DENISE

I see your reasoning; do you always care what your friends say or suggest?

RUTH

Yep, especially when they're paying for my bar tab. To tell you the truth, a cousin of Knight Rider, a biker buddy of mine, picked up your card at one of those trendy salad places.

(Ruth pauses and furrows her brow.)

Why the hell do people pay fifteen dollars for a salad is beyond me. . .. Anyway, she wanted him to give it to me and here I am.

DENISE

And I'm so glad you are; I'm here to coach you through whatever personal challenges you may be facing or just to be a nonjudgmental listener. Can you tell me a little about what you want to talk about today?

RUTH

Yeah, sure. So, yesterday I went out to my backyard and got on the old tire swing that my kids used to play on. I needed some time to think.

DENISE

I bet you had some good memories with your kids on that tire swing . . .

RUTH

Actually, it was the memories of me and my boyfriend; we had some fun on that . . . anyway, I kept swinging and swirling around and thinking about how deliciously sexy he was and then . . . I had this revelation.

(Ruth pauses.)

Everything is getting old . . . my memories, my knees, my arms, and my—

(Denise jumps in.)

DENISE

OH! Oh wait, yes, it all begins . . . the slow and steady path to a new older self.

RUTH

New older self . . . huh . . . that sounds as silly as the smelly fragrance sprays left in truck-stop bathrooms promising to destroy the odors and leaving just the scent of sunflowers.

DENISE

Umm sunflowers don't have a scent . . .

RUTH

Exactly!

DENISE

No, Ruth, I understand you are struggling; this is why you're here . . . to help ease the resistance to a natural perceived problem.

RUTH

(Ruth rolls her eyes.)

Naturally.

(Ruth pauses.)

I then realized . . .

(Ruth pauses but is putting on a brave face.)

I *want* to grow old.

DENISE

Great! Yes, growing old is a part of life.

RUTH

A part I thought I might not get to know.

DENISE

Yes, getting to know your older self is very important . . . knowing what and whom you are dealing with is halfway to understanding.

RUTH

How do you know which half needs understanding?

I'm so tired of all the self-help garbage.

(Ruth talks mockingly.)

"How to age gracefully" or "60 is the new 30" and the endless advertising . . . you too can look younger; buy our creams, use our products, and wipe age off your face in two weeks! I feel like yelling at these ladies. C'mon, just be thankful you *are* growing old!

DENISE

Umm, I'm not sure I understand.

RUTH

Yeah . . . well, ok . . . just two weeks ago, my new old man Thomas needed help to get me off the bike. I've always been a full-figured babe. Whoever said the nearer the bone, the sweeter the meat hasn't had a taste of this.

(Ruth gestures her hand over her body.)

I'm known as Baby Ruth . . . sweet and chunky. You can call me Baby if you want to.

Anyways, I felt stiff, my hips have been hurting a lot.

DENISE

Ummm, *Ruth* . . . let's take a moment and find an understanding of what you're saying and feeling. Let's go back to the swing.

Tell me what happened when you stopped swinging.

RUTH

Well . . . that's kind of . . .

(Ruth smiles sheepishly) private . . . and . . . (Ruth whispers) I'm still swinging.

DENISE

Oh no, well, I mean allegorically. . . .

RUTH

Denise you're gonna have to talk a little street if we're gonna get through this . . . alle . . . alle . . . what? Sounds more like a bad infection . . . so c'mon. I got my GED, not a PhD . . . so, please keep that in mind.

DENISE

Oh, ok, let's talk about what's bothering you today.

RUTH

(Ruth pauses.)

Imagine this, Thomas and I . . . we're riding on our bikes and up ahead we see the skies darken and the wind starts whipping. We do what every other biker usually does and find an overpass to hang out under and get our rain gear on, but deep down, I know what I'm facing; a raincoat won't help me.

DENISE

Help you with what?

RUTH

Navigating down the road of the unknown where I have no control.

DENISE

Oh . . . ok . . . you mean fate, getting older?

RUTH

I guess, in your coach's mind . . . yeah, sure. I'm getting slammed then squeezed by six decades of memories . . . some bad, like when I lost my front teeth in that god-awful dive bar, and some good. Well, good was good, let's just leave it at that . . . but that damn yesterday it's literally crushing me. I can't . . . *breathe*. I don't know who I am. How did this happen to me? *Christ!*

DENISE

Ok, Ruth, talk to me about that. Who were you and why aren't you her today?

RUTH

(Ruth isn't listening and continues to talk.)

Meanwhile it feels like I'm being dragged into tomorrow against my will. I don't wanna leave where I am, and I've lost control of my senses.

(Ruth snickers.)

Like that time at my friend's wedding when I drank too much tequila and wound up face down in their staircase-shaped wedding cake!

DENISE

Ruth let's try to find a name for this . . . road.

RUTH

What?

(Ruth nods)

(Denise rolls out the full-length mirror.)

DENISE

Ruth, I'd like you to stand in front of this mirror and look at yourself, not just look, but *see* yourself . . . as you are.

RUTH

You mean me? I know who I am.

DENISE

Ruth, yes, but just give this a try.

(Denise pauses.)

Repeat my words.

Hello, older self, I'm your younger self who refuses to let go, but really . . . I just don't know how.

RUTH

(Ruth speaks cautiously.)

Well as long as I don't have to answer to, do you swear to tell the truth the whole truth and nothing but . . .

DENISE

Try . . .

RUTH

(Ruth repeats deadpan tone.)

Hello, older self.

I'm your younger self who refuses to let go but really . . . I just don't know how.

(Ruth glances over at Denise.)

Hey coach, you know you could be a lot better looking if you . . .

(Ruth steps closer to Denise and pulls out her hairpin. Denise's hair tumbles down.)

DENISE

Oh! Ummm . . . this isn't something that should happen!

RUTH

Awww . . . c'mon, look how much better! And while we're at it . . .

(Ruth untucks her shirt partly and raises her skirt so its shorter)

There! Now, see?

(Denise is astonished but begins to look at herself and fluffs up her hair.)

Yeah, that's it! You're gonna be a back warmer in no time.

DENISE

Back warmer?

(Ruth laughs.)

RUTH

It's a friend on the back of a motorcycle.

DENISE

Honestly, you'd be surprised of what I know . . .

RUTH

Here, I want you to have this.

(Ruth takes off her bandana and puts it around Denise's head.)

You're rocking that bandana!

DENISE

But . . .

RUTH

Well . . . according to my watch, time is up!

(Ruth pauses.)

Hey Denise, I think you're a goat!

DENISE

You think I'm a farm animal?

(Ruth laughs.)

RUTH

No! Coach, I consider you the greatest of all time, a G.O.A.T. Anybody who can put up with me for thirty minutes sober is pretty damn good in my book, and wow, that's a hot look.

(Ruth looks at Denise admiringly.)

DENISE

(Denise is still taken aback with how things have transpired.)

Ok, Ruth, next week?

RUTH

Make it three; I need time to scrape up those sixty-five dollars . . . Oh . . . (Ruth talks a little slower and quietly) and I guess I was pretty good at avoiding what I really needed to talk to you about.

(Denise is looking at herself in the mirror, then glances at Ruth.)

DENISE

Ok, we can try and talk about it next time, briefly tell me what it's about?

(Ruth grows quiet and walks toward the door. Ruth then turns and looks at Denise.)

RUTH

(Ruth speaks somberly and slowly.)

You know that road? It does have a name . . . cancer . . .

(She pauses.)

It looks like you got your work cut out . . . right, coach?

DENISE

(Denise gasps, pauses, and steadily collects her emotions.)

Well . . . they don't call me the G.O.A.T. for nothing . . . and hey, I'm here for you. Anytime next week, pro bono.

RUTH

Pro bono? Remember coach about that GED.

(Ruth softly smiles.)

DENISE

(Denise pauses then smiles.)

Hey, baby . . . keep the rubber side down . . .

See ya next week?

(Ruth gives a bigger smile and tilts her head in astonishment, gives her the thumbs-up, and walks out. Denise removes the bandana and wipes her eyes.)

THE END

FORGETTING TO REMEMBER

A conversation of beaches, burgers, and holiday sales take a different turn as two friends discover the true meaning of Memorial Day.

CHARACTERS

Female – Janis - age 50+

Female – Cindy - age 50+

Female - Kathy - age 50+

Female – Tanya - age 30+

STAGE SETTING

A beauty salon waiting area.

Janis and Kathy are busy chewing gum and looking around. Cindy is thumbing through a magazine. The three are seated together next to a table with a small American flag on it.

JANIS

Oh my gosh, you should see the new bedroom set I bought . . . such a great deal. I just *love* Memorial Day sales! That's the time to get furniture for sure! I think the stores are still open on Monday, but the time to shop is now . . . besides we have to start packing for our *staycation*. The weather report for Monday looks like sunny skies! Yay!

KATHY

Yeah, I know! My grandkids are coming over. We bought this amazing grill yesterday and decided to fire it up on Monday . . . brand new and ready to go!

(Kathy shifts in her seat and looks pensive.)

Well . . . maybe I should get my husband to do a practice run on Sunday; I wouldn't want a malfunction so to speak on Monday. There will be some hangry kids if we can't grill out; they just love those baby backs . . . throw in some of my famous potato salad and BAM!

(Cindy looks up at the pair and nods in agreement.)

JANIS

Well, my husband and his family and their cousins are all coming. We've rented three cottages that's just a half a mile from the beach! It's going to be crazy fun. You should see the float I bought; when you blow it up, it looks like one big, gigantic pizza slice . . . hilarious . . . you can fit three people on the darn thing!

(Kathy takes a closer look at Janis.)

KATHY

Ha! Well, no wonder you're getting your hair colored; you don't want everyone gossiping about those graying roots!

(Janis and Kathy are laughing. Cindy looks on and just smiles. Tanya walks up and starts writing in a small notebook.)

TANYA

Hi Cindy, it won't be too much longer, Ginger is just finishing up a color. Janis, Kathy, your stylists will be free in about twenty minutes.

(They all nod in understanding and Tanya walks off.)

KATHY

Humph . . . look over there at Gladys; she thinks she's all that and then some.

JANIS

More like . . . was this and now that, eww, she should not wear those jeans!

(The pair laugh and high-five each other; Cindy looks over and half smiles.)

JANIS

(Picking at her nails.)

These damn gel nails! They crack then halfway peel off, then you gotta pick off the rest . . . or let's say . . . you try! It's all a marketing ploy; it's like the manicurists places a secret destruction mixture that's set to crack in two days after plunking down forty-five dollars plus tip! Oh my God, so stupid.

KATHY

I know! I'm thinking of going back to wearing my natural nails.

JANIS

Anyway, it's going to be so nice to just chill out and forget about the hassles of life for a while and finally just breathe and live in the moment!

KATHY

Gosh, Janis . . . you sound *weird*.

(Kathy and Janis laugh loudly and quiet down and glance over to Cindy, who is quietly sitting and looking straight ahead.)

JANIS

Oh, hey honey, I'm sorry my friend is a loudmouth!

(Kathy shoots her the side eye and they both start to laugh.)

JANIS

I'm sorry, my name is Janis, and this is Kathy. I think I've seen you here . . . what's your name?

CINDY

Cindy.

(Cindy smiles.)

JANIS

Well, we've filled your ear with our Memorial Day plans, what are you doing?

Anything special? Barbecue? Going on a vacation?

CINDY

Oh, I'll do what I always do.

(Cindy glances away and looks down.)

KATHY

Oh? Like what? I know my sister always goes to Cape Cod, but I sure as hell can't understand that. It's so crazy there on that weekend.

CINDY

Well .... The first thing I'll do is pack myself a lunch. After that I'll throw my son's old beach chair in the trunk.

JANIS

Oh yeah, I still have my son's bike. I keep telling him to come and get the darn thing and give it to my grandson, but he doesn't listen. Even when they're grown up, they don't listen . . . right?

CINDY

(Cindy shrugs and continues with her plan.)

And then I'll drive a few miles just south of here and follow the wide curve that comes to a fork in the road and turn right; that's when I start to see the red, white, and blue color of the mini flags that are placed along this road every year. Although when I was there yesterday, there were hardly *any* flags.

(Cindy pauses. Janis and Kathy are intently looking her way, each wearing a quizzical expression.)

Anyway, as I was saying, I happened upon Sam Creason, the grounds keeper, and I asked him about it, and he said that this year there weren't many volunteers, but rest assured he'd get the job done before Memorial Day somehow . . . says that's the least he could do.

(Tanya walks up.)

TANYA

Janis, could you sign in, you must have forgotten.

JANIS

Oh sure.

(Janis writes hurriedly; Tanya walks off.)

KATHY

You were saying . . .

CINDY

Oh yes . . . there's plenty of parking, so I just slow down and try my best to appreciate the peace I feel. It's all so fleeting . . . peace. Anyway, I'll park my car and before I gather my things, I'll slip off my shoes, and take a few moments to feel the morning dew under my feet and remember some of the good times I had when my son was young. (She wistfully gazes up at the ceiling.) Like when both of us would make dew angels, our equivalent to a snow angel. "Look, Mom, watch this," he would shout. "Look I'm flying." Then he would flail his arms and legs so fast in that wet grass and become a blur of bruised knees and skinny arms!

He was so full of *wonder then.*

JANIS

Oh yes . . . that's like a sand angel we make at the beach.

CINDY

Yes exactly... (She smiles gently) ... well, after a few minutes I'll gather my things and make my way toward a large lawn and then walk past the pine trees to a site surrounded by wildflowers where I'll place that old beach chair down and sit next (Cindy's voice begins to quiver) ... I'll sit next to the grave of Sgt. William Westerly, my son, where I'll once again relive the day... he died. That's a memory I'll never forget.

KATHY

(Kathy speaks gently.) I'm . . . I'm . . . I'm so sorry.

JANIS

(Janis dabs her eyes.) I . . . I . . .

CINDY

(Cindy nods their way and continues.)

When the officer came to inform me that my son had been killed in action, he wanted me to know that my son's last efforts were to protect his unit's lives and by doing so...he...lost his.

That's just his way . . . putting others before himself. It still troubles my soul to think that his last glimpse of life were the skies of a foreign country and the worried faces of his unit carrying him away. Yes, he died that day, a hero I've been told, but I've always known that. I visit him often but on Memorial Day, it's most difficult . . . remembering the words of encouragement . . . the support of the entire town . . . it all comes back, but soon like all things they . . . fade. (Cindy shakes her head and half smiles.)

(Janis and Kathy are now in disbelief. Tanya walks in smiling.)

TANYA

Cindy, your stylist is ready.

CINDY

Well . . . um . . . it was nice to meet you.

(Cindy begins to walk off.)

JANIS

WAIT!

(Cindy pauses and looks back.)

What is the name of the place where your son is laid to rest?

CINDY

Oh . . . Jackson County Veterans Memorial.

(Cindy walks off stage with Tanya; Janis and Kathy are now looking at each other. They are not smiling. Janis takes out her phone and dials.)

JANIS

Hi honey, listen, I have something very important.

(Janis pauses.)

NO! Forget the ribs and sodas, please . . . just call Jackson County Veterans Memorial and . . .

(There is another pause.)

YES, that's what I said . . . Jackson County Veterans Memorial and ask for Mr. Creason; let him know we're stopping by today to help out.

(She pauses.)

Honey, I know we had plans to finish the shopping . . . forget it; we have something more important. . . . Oh, I'll explain when I get home.

(Kathy is shaking her head in agreement and they hold hands; Kathy calls out to Tanya.)

KATHY

Hey Tanya, we'll call for another appointment...something more important came up!

(Janis and Kathy wave toward the direction where Tanya and Cindy went. Janis and Kathy pause momentarily, lock arms, and walk out. Lights are still on for about 15 seconds, then fade to dark.

THE END

THE CLEANSER

*A granddaughter searching for her grandmother at a psychic fair
receives some unexpected grandfatherly advice.*

CHARACTERS

Female- Clara, the psychic - age 40+

Elderly Female -Grandmother - age 75+

Female -Granddaughter Zuzanna (pronounced Zu-za-na-na) age
30+

STAGE SETTING

A psychic parlor.

Clara, the psychic, is sitting at her table shuffling a deck of cards and
moving around various stones on the table. An elderly woman peers
through the door and walks with her cane up to Clara.

GRANDMOTHER

Is this where I find the aura cleaner?

(Walking with an oversized purse and clacking her cane up to the table where Clara is sitting).

CLARA

Well, really, I clear auras.

GRANDMOTHER

That's what I said, I'd like to buy some of that aura cleaner. Where are the shelves and (she sniffs twice) what is that terrible smell?

CLARA

Oh! It's patchouli and it's used for—

GRANDMOTHER

Well, somebody better clean that up; it might leave a stain so bad, you have to run it down to the river and give it a good scrubbing with borax.

CLARA

Uhm, no, it's not . . . never mind. (She is flustered.)

Why don't you go try past lives? It's only two doors down. (She said with fake cheerfulness.)

GRANDMOTHER

Oh, hell no! I just left the past! My spirit won't let me go all the way back there. Now I would like to try some aura cleaner on my floors; I can't get them clean.

CLARA

I'm sorry I don't sell floor cleaner; however, if your aura needs cleansing, I'm your girl.

GRANDMOTHER

I see, doesn't aura mean floor in Spanish?

CLARA

(Clara says a little irritated.)

I'll have to Google that!

GRANDMOTHER

(Picks up the oversized magnifying glass on the table.)

What in the world is this for?

CLARA

Please don't touch that. (The woman puts it down.) I use it to read palms.

GRANDMOTHER

(The woman pulls out a chair and sits down.)

Aww . . . you use it to read Psalms too? I think that's my favorite in the Old Testament, and I understand why you use it; the words are pretty darn small.

CLARA

No, that's not . . . (Clara mutters underneath her breath.) Are you lost? Tell me your name so that I can get you some help.

GRANDMOTHER

My name? Umm . . . ummm . . .

ZUZANNA

(Zuzanna peeks through the door) Bubbe! I've been looking all over for you!

GRANDMOTHER

(The grandmother looks at Clara) My name is Bubbe... (She turns to her granddaughter)

I was simply looking for floor cleaner and this nice lady was going to help me read the . . .

ZUZANNA

It's ok, Bubbe, I've been looking all over for you, scared me half to death! I asked you to stay in the car.

GRANDMOTHER

But . . .

ZUZANNA

(Zunzanna yells toward stage side to John who is not seen)

John, I found her; please come take her to the car.

(Zuzanna walks toward her confused grandmother, takes her hand and leads her offstage to John)

Don't worry, Bubbe, everything is going to be alright.

GRANDMOTHER

I know, dear, just don't forget the floor cleaner.

ZUZANNA

I will, Bubbe, now go with John.

(Once she hands her grandmother offstage, she approaches Clara with anger)

Whatever your fee is I will settle it, but you of all people should know that it is bad karma to take advantage of a mentally disabled old woman!

CLARA

(Clara is shocked and stands up.) I never took advantage of your grandmother, she wandered into my space looking for floor cleaner. I could tell she was confused, and something wasn't right, but I would never harm her in any way, so you don't owe me anything. And if you'll excuse me, my next appointment is due any minute. (She starts shuffling the things on the table around.)

ZUZANNA

You know, it all happened so fast. One minute we're laughing and joking, shopping, cooking together. Then it was, as if someone flipped a switch and her memory began to flicker like a flame losing oxygen. Sometimes she doesn't know who I am; the doctors have not given her much time.

Anyway, I'm sorry for the accusation and . . . thank you.

CLARA

You're welcome and I'm sorry about all of this.

ZUZANNA

Ok ... bye. (Zuzanna walks towards the door and Clara calls out to her)

CLARA

Wait!!

(Zuzanna stops and turns around)

CLARA

Can you please come back, and have a seat for a moment, please? I have something to share with you.

ZUZANNA

Ok, but I only have a few minutes, I'll text my husband and let him know.

(Zuzanna takes out her phone and sends a text message.)

Ok, I just told him to take grandma to the ice cream shop that's two doors down.

CLARA

(Clara takes a deep breath and exhales.) I'm hearing a message that I need to tell ... it's (she struggles with words) che ... ch ... just a minute; this one is difficult ... I'm not familiar with the language. (She concentrates hard.) *Czesc piekna* ... there, that's it *Czesc piekna*. Do you recognize this?

ZUZANNA

(Zuzanna sits down with a shocked expression on her face.)

How do you know these words?

CLARA

There is someone who just said them to me . . . to say to you.

ZUZANNA

This is impossible!

CLARA

So, you know what it means and who it is from? I don't even know what language this is.

ZUZANNA

(Zuzanna speaks in a hushed tone,)

It's Polish; it means "Hello, beautiful." Those are the words my grandfather would say to me when I came home from school.

CLARA

(Clara takes a breath and exhales.) Zu . . . Zuza . . . I don't know . . .

ZUZANNA

Zuzanna . . . that's my name.

CLARA

There is a man holding a bouquet of red poppies.

ZUZANNA

Zeyde . . . Grandpa?

CLARA

Yes, he sends his love to you, and he says please try not to cry so much for your grandmother.

ZUZANNA

I . . . I don't believe in these things!

CLARA

I understand but ... I can't control who comes to me or what I need to hear or say to someone. All I know is that ... wait ... (She closes her eyes) He is showing me a fiddle.

ZUZANNA

(Zuzanna is astonished.) It must be!

CLARA

He says for you to take your grandmother to the park near your home; let her take all the time she wants. . .. It's a place where she finds peace.

ZUZANNA

I know where it is; I really need to leave now.

CLARA

I know this is difficult for you; it just happened . . . wait . . . please don't go. There is one more thing . . . your grandfather is smiling. He said that you were always the sensitive one and that's what makes you special . . . your empathy . . . but for you to continue with your writings about our past . . . and how we not only survived but thrived.

Ummm, let me try. . . . *Badz siena mojo corko.* (She takes a breath and exhales.) Did you understand what I said?

ZUZANNA

Yes, he said . . . (she gets emotional) he said . . . be strong my granddaughter.

CLARA

Well, that's all I can hear now. I'm just as taken aback as you, like I said, I don't really have control over that. It's a part of my gift. Can you talk to me about your writings?

ZUZANNA

(Zuzanna gets up and speaks.) Yes, I can . . . You see, my maternal grandparents were some of the few that were liberated from Auschwitz. After Granddad passed away, the weight of those memories of hundreds of skeletal like people standing in ashes of their loved ones fell on my grandmother. Before the disease consumed her, she and I spent many nights holding each other while she recalled those horrible crimes. We vowed we would continue on with our book knowing that there are those who deny it ever happened . . . but it did.

CLARA

Zuzanna, you have been blessed with the understanding of how fragile life can be. I know it will be difficult, but your grandmother's goodbye will be your grandfather's hello and the eternal peace they so deserve is not far away. Do you have a title for the book?

ZUZANNA

Yes, when the disease began to consume her, she would say at random times: *"What is over there?"*

CLARA

Oh? I'm hearing this as a rhetorical question of some kind. Was she able to explain it at all?

ZUZANNA

(Zuzanna shakes her head no.)

No, but while speaking with other survivors from that time, it was told to me that one of the first questions asked of the liberators was "What's over there?" as they pointed northward toward a cluster of trees in the distance . . . to which the liberators replied . . . camps. The questions were simple but complex in their bewilderment; freedom seemed to be just outside those fences, or so they thought. Therefore, the working title is "What's Over There?" A survival story of fences and fire.

CLARA

I do see this being a novel for the ages, and hope that you continue with your grandfather's encouragement and if you need someone to talk to, call me anytime. (Clara gives her card to Zuzanna.)

ZUZANNA

Dziekuje . . . thank you. (She manages a brief smile and leaves.)

CLARA

(Clara contemplates what just happened and reaches for her cell phone.)

Hi, Ma. (She pauses.) You're going to work in your garden tomorrow? Great, I can bring my gloves and help you. (She laughs.) No, Mom, my wanting to spend time with you is not because I've had a vision. I just want to say I love you and would like some mother-daughter time, no ulterior motives . . . ok . . . see you soon. (She hangs up, holding phone in her hand, and closes her eyes as if meditating and the light fades.)

THE END

FAITH RENEWED

A mother rediscovers the power of prayer and faith.

CHARACTERS

Female - Carly Sanders - age 19

Female - Ms. Sanders - age 40+

Male - Dr. Jennings - age 50+

Male - Pastor Carlson - age 70+

STAGE SETTING

A hospital bed.

Carly Sanders is somewhat sedated with black charcoal liquid on her mouth and on her hospital gown. Dr. Jennings stands outside the door waiting for Ms. Sanders to arrive.

(Ms. Sanders runs up to Dr. Jennings frantically.)

MS. SANDERS

How is she? Where is she? What happened?

DR. JENNINGS

We have her sedated but whatever she has taken is still in her system; we have to keep a very close watch. She's in here.

(Dr. Jennings gestures toward the hospital bed. Ms. Sanders peers in and shrieks)

MS. SANDERS

Oh my God! What is that stuff coming out of her mouth?

(Ms. Sanders covers her face in grief.)

DR. JENNINGS

Don't worry, Ms. Sanders; it's just the activated charcoal we are using to possibly help absorb noxious substances that may have been ingested, including certain types of drugs.

MS. SANDERS

DRUGS? My daughter doesn't use drugs! She's an honor student! A really good kid!

DR. JENNINGS

Ms. Sanders, the usage of drugs has infiltrated all walks of life; please this isn't the time nor the place to discuss such matters. Your daughter is exhibiting hallucinations, in and out of consciousness, and her heart rate is dangerously low. I want you to know that we're doing all that we can.

MS. SANDERS

(She inches up to the bedside and speaks softly; the doctor backs away.)

Carly? Carly? It's Mom; I'm here. You're going to be ok.

(Carly is now moving around in the bed and opens her eyes.)

CARLY

(Carly shouts.) GO AWAY, YOU MONSTER!

(The mother backs away in disbelief.)

MS. SANDERS

Oh my God, my daughter! She doesn't recognize me!

(Ms. Sander's voice now rises.)

I want a priest! Doesn't this hospital have a priest?!

DR. JENNINGS

Ms. Sanders please calm your voice; I'll go call for our hospital chaplain.

(Dr. Jennings has momentarily left and Ms. Sanders talks to herself while looking up)

MS. SANDERS

Oh, now I ask for some religious guy! God . . . Jesus . . . whoever you are . . . (she's wringing her hands) I must be desperate! Oh, the great wizard in the sky . . . who believes that crap . . . it's no use. Even if there was a Jesus, why in the hell would he even give a rip about me. (She sighs heavily.)

(In walks Dr. Jennings.)

DR. JENNINGS

Ms. Sanders, this is our hospital chaplain, Pastor Carlson.

PASTOR CARLSON

Ms. Sanders? I understand you are in need of prayer.

MS. SANDERS

Oh, you're the priest? (Ms. Sanders looks shocked.) Aren't you supposed to be wearing a cross or something? You look more like some random grandpa wandering the grocery aisle, looking for denture cleaner. I don't need your prayer; my daughter does!

Please!!!

(Ms. Sanders takes the priest by the arm and guides him to Carly's bedside.

Carly is writhing, groaning loudly and pounding her fists on the bed. The priest's eyes widen in shock and he appears to be frightened)

PASTOR CARLSON

Wha . . . what do you want me to do?

MS. SANDERS

(Ms. Sanders says clearly annoyed.)

What do you mean? You're a preacher! Do what you preachers do and get in there and PRAY! Jesus Christ!

PASTOR CARLSON

(Pastor Carlson is now shaking a little but keeps a coolness about him. Carly has now grown still. They slowly approach the bedside.

Pastor Carlson reaches in his pocket and gets his Bible out, opens it, and begins to pray.)

Dear Heavenly Father, we ask you to place your healing hands on—

CARLY

(She snaps up and gets in Pastor Carlson's face and yells.)

GO TO HELL!

(Pastor Carlson is now in a panic and shuts his Bible and quickly backs away.)

(He speaks quickly and does the sign of the cross.)

—and thank you, Heavenly Father, for your mercy AMEN.

(Pastor Carlson is now walking briskly away from the room. Ms. Sanders chases him down and grabs his arm.)

MS. SANDERS

Get back in there! You mean to tell me that's all you're going to do? My daughter is dying!

(Ms. Sanders is now pacing nervously near Pastor Carlson.)

PASTOR CARLSON

(Pastor Carlson breathes heavily.)

Prayer works by welcoming more of God's power to flow through our lives, and Ms. Sanders, I will keep you in my prayers as well.

MS. SANDERS

(Ms. Sanders says frustrated.)

But nothing's changed! She's still flailing and crying; nothing's changed! I thought prayers worked!

PASTOR CARLSON

I've done all I can do, Ms. Sanders, the rest is up to God. Now if you will excuse me, I have other patients to attend to. Please, Ms. Sanders, He's God.... He hears us and will intercede in his time.

MS. SANDERS

I don't believe you!

PASTOR CARLSON

It's not me; you have to believe. (He looks up and gently gestures upward.) It's Him that you need to believe.

(Pastor Carlson exits, leaving Ms. Sanders. Seconds have passed and Carly is lying still. The Dr enters and checks her pulse and writes in her chart, and the doctor approaches Ms. Sanders.)

DR. JENNINGS

Ms. Sanders, we've done all we can for now; we just have to wait and see. She is stable but it's still unclear if her cognitive abilities have been affected. Once I receive the lab results then I will know if further treatment is required. Police have reported that people are making brownies baked with mushrooms laced with some LSD.

MS. SANDERS

(Ms. Sanders sounds dejected.)

What? Oh No! Oh my gosh . . . at least ... Can I stay with her?

DR. JENNINGS

Sure, but Ms. Sanders, any unnecessary outburst will only make things worse. The staff is just outside with our monitoring system.

(Ms. Sanders slowly walks toward her daughter, who is lying very still. She takes her hand and begins to softly sob.)

MS. SANDERS

Ok, I can do this . . . my Carly.

Oh God, she is so sweet; she's been so good to me. She always sent me Mother's Day cards, cooked for me, bought me those cozy silver slippers . . . God, I know I haven't bothered with you, and I'm not sure when that happened, but God (she kisses her daughter's hand), if you can look over the fact, I once took five dollars from the collection plate, that one time, and really see my heart, please God, help her get out of this . . . please.

(She barely can get the word "please" out and she places her head on her daughter's chest.)

CARLY

(Carly awakens and speaks in a tired, shocked voice.)

Mom, did you really steal from the collection plate?

And can you get your head off my chest; I can't really breathe? (She coughs and her mom's head pops up in surprise.)

MS. SANDERS

Oh, Carly! You know me! That's great! Oh, Caaaarly!

CARLY

(Carly speaks weakly.)

Of course, I know you. Are you feeling ok?

(She coughs a little.)

Where are we? What's going on?

(Just then the doctor comes in.)

DR. JENNINGS

(Dr. Jennings grabs Carly's wrist and checks her pulse.)

Welcome back, young lady, you had us all worried.

Your pulse is normal. I will order some new tests to make sure you're ok.

CARLY

I don't know what to say except thank you.

DR. JENNINGS

Carly, you do know why you're in the hospital.

CARLY

Yeah, I think so. I was hanging out with my friends after school and remember eating a brownie that Lisa said she made especially for me. It looked good and smelled good, so I ate it.

MS. SANDERS

How could Lisa do such a cruel thing to you?

DR. JENNINGS

Well, as your doctor, my main concern is your health but as a concerned parent of my own teenage daughter, I highly recommend that you and your mother have a talk about how to proceed from here, and she can have a little broth, it might help soothe her stomach. (He exits the room.)

CARLY

I'm so sorry, Mom.

MS. SANDERS

It's not your fault, Carly, but remember you are who your friends are and you're better than this. In two months, you're headed to college; your whole life is ahead of you.

CARLY

You're right, Mom, and rest assured, it will be a long time before I eat another brownie . . . if ever. (They laugh.)

MS. SANDERS

Well, let me go get that broth for you. I'll be right back. (Carly nods her head. Ms. Sanders steps away. A spotlight now illuminates Ms. Sanders, who looks skyward and mouths a thank you and a reverent nod.)

(Spotlight slowly fades from the illuminated smiling face of Ms. Sanders.)

THE END

MY FLOWER

The missing piece of a woman's identity is revealed in an unlikely place.

CHARACTERS

Female - Therapist - age 60+

Asian female - Julie Jenkins - age 40+

Asian man - Kiyoshi - age 60+

Homeless Male - age 50+

STAGE SETTING

Stage right has a desk, lamp, and two chairs.

Stage left is a park bench.

The scene opens with stage right illuminating the therapist office.

THERAPIST

Julie, we're almost out of time. Is there anything else you want to talk about?

JULIE

(Julie is sobbing quietly.) Well . . . yes . . . my . . . my *dooooooog!*

THERAPIST

Your dog?

JULIE

Yes . . . she died! She . . . was hit by a car in the mountains when we were on vacation, and we had to leave her there.

THERAPIST

Oh, I'm really sorry . . . when?

JULIE

When I was five!

(Julie cries into her hands.)

THERAPIST

Oh, I see. Julie, it's encouraging to me to know that you are now attempting to heal your past. Remember when we talked about reconciling with your past?

JULIE

So awful . . . and why did they say those things?

(Julie now stands.)

(She screams.) BUCK TOOTH, MONKEY EARS, JAPANESE *JULIE!*

THERAPIST

Oh no, Julie, please sit back down and explain this. I think you were bullied.

JULIE

Huh! Try listening to that every day. As you know my parents placed me in a private school and I still felt ... like a piece ... of a puzzle that's missing ... an ... unfinished feeling.

THERAPIST

I understand, but sometimes those who are different in how they look or even their academic successes can create a certain animosity. I know your parents would be so proud of your accomplishments if they were alive today.

JULIE

Yeah, maybe if they were alive today, they could've helped me understand where I came from. They tried but I would just cover my ears when I was a kid so after some time, they dropped it. Being adopted is a moniker I can't escape.

(Julie grows reflective.)

I've come to terms with their reasoning; they loved me so very much ... I know that.

THERAPIST

Julie, you are becoming very strong in your understanding, we'll work on techniques to help calm your emotions next visit. I'll see you in two weeks.

JULIE

(Julie has a feeling of being depleted.)

Ok, thank you, and oh, I'll continue reading that book you loaned me on coming to terms with who you are and who you can become. Thank you.

(Julie walks out. Stage lights go out on therapist office and stage lights now illuminate the park bench where Julie decides to sit despite a homeless man lying nearby. An elderly man walks up to her.)

KIYOSHI

May I sit here?

JULIE

Sure.

(Julie glances in his direction and straightens her posture and gazes off to the other side)

KIYOSHI

Nice day, isn't it?

JULIE

(Julie looks at Kiyoshi, who is now staring intently at Julie's face.)

Yes, it is ummm . . .

(There is a moment where they are looking directly at each other. Kiyoshi breaks the gaze and looks away. Julie goes back to a daydreaming state, looking off toward the horizon. Kiyoshi looks down and begins to weep. He reaches for a tissue from his pocket and dabs his eyes and quietly weeps that doesn't go unnoticed by Julie. Her facial expression changes from dreamy to concerned and she turns toward Kiyoshi.)

JULIE

Hey, is there something wrong? Can I call someone? Are you ok?

(Kiyoshi now looks up and into Julie's eyes.)

KIYOSHI

You have your mother's eyes.

(Kiyoshi looks down and continues softly weeping.)

JULIE

(Julie now looks confused.)

What? What did you say?

KIYOSHI

You . . . have . . . your mother's eyes.

JULIE

(Julie is confused and squirms.)

You . . . mean . . . you knew my mother, Marla Jenkins?

KIYOSHI

No, not the mother you have known, but the mother who brought you into this life.

(Julie is now edging herself away and begins to stand.)

JULIE

I . . . I . . . have to go; I'm sure you are mistaken. I . . . I . . . can't . . .

KIYOSHI

WAIT! Please stay; I am sorry. Please . . . stay a moment.

(Julie slowly sinks back down on the bench, never taking her eyes off Kiyoshi.)

I didn't expect you to sit here, the very bench that I sat on many times and watched you grow. My heart told me to come to you and begin a journey that must be made. I have come to know that there is no good time and there is no bad time to conquer your fear.

JULIE

Journey? What . . . what do you mean?

KIYOSHI

I have lived a full life in America. I have been taught well in its customs and language and have embraced them as my own. I have had a long journey and relished the beauty of knowledge but there is one path on this journey that I have longed for . . . the most important one . . . the path that has led me to you.

JULIE

(Julie is looking confused and interested.)

Me? What do you mean...me?

KIYOSHI

(Kiyoshi speaks Japanese, then English.)

Watashi wa anata no chichioyadesu . . . I am your father.

(Julie has a look of astonishment and places her hand on her head.)

JULIE

What? I . . . I think I'm going to faint.

(Kiyoshi grabs her hand.)

KIYOSHI

No . . . no . . . I'm sorry . . . please have patience. I know this is so much . . . don't run! Don't leave . . .

(Julie collects her emotions and swallows hard and takes a deep breath.)

JULIE

My *father?*

(Julie now raises her hand toward Kiyoshi's face and begins to see herself in astonishment for the first time.)

I . . . ooh . . . I . . . see . . . *me.*

KIYOSHI

I am so sorry; I know a park bench is not suitable for such an announcement, but my heart compelled me forward . . . and now we are here. I have always followed the wisdom of the soul and . . .

(Kiyoshi begins to weep.)

I knew it would bring me to this day.

(Julie moves closer to Kiyoshi with a look of bewilderment.)

I know you have many questions. There are so many things to tell you but first there is something I have waited a thousand lifetimes to say to you.

(Julie and Kiyoshi are looking directly at each other. Kiyoshi is now sobbing.)

Watashi wa anata o aishiteimasu watashi no hana . . . I *love* you, my flower.

(Julie is stunned and grabs his hand.)

When you were born, the first thing your mother whispered to you was *Sakura . . . Watashi no utsukushi musume.* Sakura, my *beautiful* daughter. She saw the strength of the cherry blossom tree in you the moment you came into this world. I had no idea she was going to bestow this name on you . . . I was so pleased.

JULIE

(Julie repeats in a whisper.)

Sakura . . .

(Kiyoshi is now looking down and weeps.)

KIYOSHI

When your mother died, I began to fall behind with basic survival supplies. The bombs may have stopped falling from the sky, but pain, disease, and hardships kept raining. Americans were now visiting our towns, offering to take our children and raise them as their own. I met the couple who came for you, they were honorable and kind.

(Kiyoshi dabs his eyes and continues.)

I lifted you up into their arms and they walked toward the waiting car. You reached for me . . . *chichioya* . . . *chichioya* . . . father . . . father . . . and just before they entered the car, the wind lifted your hair for a brief moment, and I saw your tear-streaked face. Overcome with grief, I fell to the ground; when I came to, you were gone . . .

(Kiyoshi sobs.)

. . . *gone.*

(There is a brief moment of silence.)

JULIE

Well, I am here, and you are here.

(Julie outstretches her arms and whispers.)

Chichioya . . . chichioya . . .

(Julie and Kiyoshi fall into each other's arms. The sound of crying is now audible. A surprised Julie and Kiyoshi pause and look startled.)

HOMELESS MAN

(The homeless man is crying.)

That's the most beautiful story I've ever heard in all my days lying here!

(The homeless man dabs his eyes with the tail of his shirt and sniffs. The trio now share a small heartfelt laugh and quizzically look at each other.)

KIYOSHI

We must partake in Omatsuri, a festival of gratitude! I will take you.

(Kiyoshi gestures at the homeless man and smiles.)

And *you please come* with us.

HOMELESS MAN

(The man is smiling broadly.)

Ok, I never tasted Omatsuri, but I'll try it!

(Kiyoshi just shakes his head and smiles as they all walk off stage arm in arm laughing.)

Lights go dark.

THE END

THE WEDDING

As a romantic gesture, the groom decides to take his unsuspecting bride to the woods where they fell in love before going to their reception.

CHARACTERS

Male - Joshua - age 20+

Female - Alice - age 20+

Male - Tom - age 20+

STAGE SETTING

A rickety, homemade, weathered wooden bench.

(Bride emerges from stage left. Bride heads toward bench in her vintage wedding gown and sits down in a huff. The groom in his tuxedo comes in seconds later with a bag containing two plastic champagne glasses and a bottle of champagne. They are both very dirty from walking in the woods; she has leaves and sticks stuck in her hair.)

JOSHUA

Ahhhh . . . honey, I'm sorry!

ALICE

Sorry? Well, you should be! What were you thinking? I told you we were going to be late for the reception! Nobody is going to know where we are! Oh my God! REALLY?

JOSHUA

I wanted to sneak you away for just a little bit and have you to myself; I had something to say to you . . . you know before all the crazy happens . . .

ALICE

Before all the crazy happens?

What in the hell do you call this?

I'm sitting on a worn-out, moss-covered bench in the middle of the woods on my wedding day. To make matters worse, my grandma's cherished vintage dress now has brand-new rips to add to the charm mixed with the color of . . . of . . . *mud*!!! My something old has turned into my something AWFUL!

JOSHUA

Mi amor . . . calm down! (The groom pleads with her while he puts down the bag.)

ALICE

Don't tell me to calm down . . . and by the way . . . THIS IS CALM!

JOSHUA

Well, I guess you wondered why I took the Jeep to drive to the reception.

ALICE

Well, it did cross my mind, but I had other things I was thinking about . . . like getting to the reception. We have everyone waiting! The DJ is paid by the hour and if I remember correctly, he's already been there two hours!

(Alice tries her phone again.)

Darn it . . . no reception here.

JOSHUA

When I misjudged the depth of that old water hole and we stalled out, you left like the wind! You didn't give me a chance to explain.

ALICE

EXPLAIN? Joshua! It's my wedding day.

JOSHUA

Alice . . . it's *our* wedding day.

(Alice now has her arms crossed and her back to him. Joshua gets up, walks around, and stands in her line of vision.)

JOSHUA

For your information, if you'll listen to me, I handed my best man (he smiles) a note, telling him where we are and why we were going to be late. I'm sure by now someone, most likely he, will be here soon. (His voice trails off.)

ALICE

Oh, you mean the worst best man ever! He's probably hitting on the server from the Crooked Inn you hired to help with the bar at our wedding.

JOSHUA

Yeah, you're probably right, but he's really a great guy Alice. You just haven't warmed up to him.

ALICE

Well, maybe, Josh, it's got something to do with every time you two get together, mischief follows. You remember your mug shot? Both of you had black eyes because he thought it would be funny to drag you onstage during the stripper show at your bachelor party, causing you to get roughed up by the bouncers! Oh, nice keepsake that mug shots going to be . . . can't wait to show . . . to . . . show . . . that to . . . our *children!!!*

(Alice begins to tear up.)

And then not five months ago, you two "went fishing" and ended up at some dive bar that you tried to moor up to but instead you crashed into their dock, costing us thousands of dollars! It's a good thing the bartender's daughter *knew* Tom and smoothed it all over when the cops showed up.

JOSHUA

Welllllll . . . one day you'll see the guy I've known for the past ten years . . . let's forget about that.

(Joshua kneels now and takes her hand.)

ALICE

Josh...nobody knows where...

JOSHUA

Ok, stop a minute . . . you do remember this spot . . . right?

This bench we built together is still here solid, just like our love for each other.

ALICE

(Alice rolls her eyes.)

Yes.

You were so cute.

JOSHUA

Cute? I think I'm rather handsome. (He laughs.)

(He gestures to himself.) Especially in this tux. As for that explanation as to why we are here . . . (He pulls out the flutes and champagne, pours and places bottle down and hands a flute to Alice.)

I wanted this moment for just us, here where it all began.

(He clears throat.)

Alice, I knew the moment I saw you take those old hiking boots off and stretch out on our campsite last August in that other clearing right down there. . ..

(Joshua gestures to the side.)

I knew at that moment that I wanted to spend the rest of my life feeling your warmth against me while we watch the stars at night.

(He pauses.)

You remind me so much of this forest . . . so . . .

mysterious and untamed . . . . . .as we stand among these beautiful pines...I pledge my eternal love...to my wife...

(Joshua looks at Alice and raises his glass she gingerly raises hers. They intertwine hands and only Joshua takes a drink, she quickly puts her drink on the bench)

ALICE

Well, why in the hell didn't you say something, you crazy fool!!

(She takes his drink and puts it on the bench beside hers and then wraps her arms around his neck)

JOSHUA

And spoil a surprise for a wife who apparently doesn't do well with surprises?

(Joshua laughs.)

ALICE

You're not the only one who has a surprise . . . although this isn't the place I had in mind.

JOSHUA

Ummm . . . Alice, (he laughs nervously) what are you talking about.

ALICE

(She places her hands on her abdomen.)

Joshua . . . what I'm trying to say is that . . . we're pregnant!

JOSHUA

Pre . . . pre (he's hardly breathing) . . . pregnant?

ALICE

Yes, Joshua! You're going to be a father!

JOSHUA

(He falls to his knees at the level of her belly and gets emotional) What can I say?

ALICE

How about *Hola mi bambino Eres tu Papi*? We'll teach her both our languages.

JOSHUA

Oh my God! (He touches her belly.) *Hola mi bambino eres tu papi.* . .. (He stands up and wipes his eyes.) Alice . . . this is the best day of my life. First, I marry the most beautiful woman I've ever known and now she tells me she's having our baby! Alice . . . Alice, uh-oh, I feel . . . (He faints.)

TOM

Alice! Joshua! Can you hear me?

ALICE

Over here, Tom . . . over here.

(Tom comes running toward them and sees Joshua on the ground.)

ALICE

He ... fain—

TOM

Nobody panic! I know CPR!!!

(He drops down toward Joshua, who is groaning as Tom tries to perform CPR.)

JOSHUA

Naw, man, I'm ok. (Joshua pushes Tom away.) Sheesh, I thought you gave up drinking whiskey ... help me up. (Tom helps him stand up.)

TOM

What happened here?

ALICE

Apparently, I have a husband who doesn't do well with surprises.

TOM

Oh, yeah? Well, what's the surprise?

JOSHUA

We'll tell you later. It's been a long day and I guess I haven't eaten.

TOM

I got worried ... I found that note you gave me when I went to tip that hottie bartender and let everyone know you were going to be late. After an hour, a group of us decided to come looking for you guys. I saw your Jeep back there and freaked out.

(Tom stops and looks at Alice.)

Alice, you are so beautiful! Josh, you're a lucky man! But you knew that . . . remember that first date I told you she was the one? Alice, I never told you, but I'm sorry I dragged Josh into those big messes. He told me how mad you were, so I want to make my own promise and request if I could.

ALICE

(Alice glances skeptically at Tom.)

Ok . . . sure.

TOM

Alice, I promise that I won't drag Josh on anymore stripper stages and no more crazy antics. And if you could find it in your heart. Will you name your firstborn after me . . . even if it's a girl? Well, if it's a girl, Thomasina?

ALICE

(Alice and Joshua look at each other and laugh heartily.)

We'll have to think about that one, Tom.

TOM

Hey, we have a search party. I know where they are. Joshua, you know the place, just past that big rock by the bend in the river. Let's get on over there, besides we got a reception to attend, and my, my, that server you hired, Josh . . .

(Tom whistles and gives the thumbs-up to Josh. Alice rolls her eyes and grabs onto Joshua, then Joshua grabs Tom and they exit together laughing.)

THE END

THE LETTER

CHARACTERS

Black Female-Loretta Williams - age 16+

Black Female-Ester Williams - age 50+

Black Male dressed in uniform and white gloves-Honor Guard - age 20+

Black Male dressed in uniform and white gloves-Honor Guard - age 20+

Black Male-Pastor Franklin - age 70+

Black Male-Military Representative of the Armed Forces - age 40+

STAGE SETTING

On far right of stage isolated with spotlight is a casket that has an American flag draped over it, the casket is positioned so that the audience cannot see inside it. The chairs are positioned near the casket. On the far left in the darkened area is a podium. A folded flag to present to the family.

Ester Williams, her daughter Loretta, and the Military Representative, who is holding a satchel containing a letter, are standing away from the casket but still in the light.

NARRATOR

This play is dedicated to the memory of the deadliest stateside disaster of World War II, an accidental explosion on July 17, 1944, at Port Chicago, CA, that killed hundreds of men, the majority of them black. Although the characters in this play are fictitious, it allows us to examine a part of history that remains unknown to many. Under the threat of death, many sailors returned to work but some of them did not, they were known as the Port Chicago 50. They stood for their beliefs and eventually their actions paved the way for the desegregation of the Navy and helped shore up safer working conditions. Despite their impact on our armed forces, The Port Chicago Naval Magazine Memorial is one of the least visited sites in the National Park's service system.

MILITARY REPRESENTATIVE

(He speaks calmly, quietly.)

Mrs. Williams, I have this satchel that belonged to your son. I wanted to personally give it to you. It was found in the rubble several days after the explosion. I felt it was too valuable to send through the postal service.

(He hands the satchel with a letter inside to Ester; she takes it slowly.)

ESTER

Thank you, sir.

(Ester places the satchel around her shoulder)

MILITARY REPRESENTATIVE

I understand you want to see your son but given the extent of his facial injuries, I don't think it's—

ESTER

I want to *see* my son! I birthed him in this world and I'm going to see him out so, please . . . Loretta, honey, you don't have to go any closer.

LORETTA

(Loretta's voice is shaking.)

Mom, I told you I'm going he's, *my* brother. When Dad passed, he took me in his arms and promised to always see about me, and now I'm going to see about him.

(Loretta begins to cry; they both have tissues in their hand.)

MILITARY REPRESENTATIVE

(He speaks softly.)

Ok, Mrs. Williams, we'll be just outside; we have about fifteen minutes before we gather.

(The military representative walks into the dark side of stage, leaving them alone. Ester and Loretta hold hands, clinging to one another they slowly approach the casket.)

ESTER

Loretta, you stay right here; I want to go first, please . . . just stay here.

(Ester lets go of her hand and takes in a deep, apprehensive breath and approaches, then peers into the casket)

ESTER

(Ester sobs loudly.)

They made a mistake!!! This is *not* my son!

(Ester turns her head and sobs.)

LORETTA

MOM! Stop . . .

(Ester grabs her hand and pulls her in for an embrace.)

They told us that his wounds were . . .

ESTER

I . . . I . . .

(Ester turns back to the casket, this time with Loretta. Loretta peers in and let's go of her mother's hand.)

LORETTA

Mom . . .

(Loretta sobs loudly. Ester comes closer to Loretta and looks again; this time she grows pensive.)

ESTER

Yes . . .

(Ester is whispering; Loretta continues to sob and is still looking away.)

Yes . . . the jawline . . . his nose . . . oh no . . . God, no! Darnell!

(Ester and Loretta embrace and sob. Ester blindly reaches for her tissue and brushes up against the satchel.)

ESTER

Loretta (she can barely catch her breath), this is his, this is Darnell's. I want to see what's in it.

(Loretta is still sobbing.)

LORETTA

Mom, are you sure . . .? Let's go we've seen him. I can't take it anymore.

(Ester still is sobbing; she opens the satchel and notices an unopened letter with her address on it.)

ESTER

Look, Loretta, this letter is to me. . .. It . . . it was never sent.

(Ester opens the letter, looks at the first line, and crumples it against her chest.)

LORETTA

Mom . . . read it . . . (Loretta dabs her eyes and continues, her voice shaking) to me too.

ESTER

(Ester takes a breath, sighs, and begins.)

"Dear Mom,

It's already July 16th! I'm surprised at how fast 1944 is moving; time sure goes by fast even if you're not having fun.

(Ester pauses for a moment and continues.)

I know it's been some time since my last letter, but I've been busy with all the loading. It's dangerous work, but, Mom, you raised me to be strong and face my obstacles with a healthy dose of heavenly humbleness. I never knew what that meant until recently . . .

(Ester pauses; Loretta rubs her back for a moment.)

There's a lot of pressure on our shoulders here at Port Chicago, so I rely on brute strength as well as that inner strength you kept telling me about; in fact, my superiors always bet on me; they know I'm the fastest, strongest loader they got!

(Ester looks away and dabs her eyes. She continues with a quivering voice.)

How's Loretta doing? Tell her I have my eagle eyes on her; she knows what I mean. Be sure to ask her about those eagles that fly over our farm from time to time."

LORETTA

He always loved birds . . . all kinds . . .

ESTER

Yes, he sure did.

LORETTA

(Loretta gently places her hand on her mother's shoulder.)

Are you ok to go on Mom?

ESTER

Yes, I am. (Ester clears her throat and continues.)

"I always point at it, and I say, Loretta, see that eagle; that's going to be me! I'm going to soar so high some day and be the man Dad always wanted me to be! She always liked that part. I sure miss him, Mom, and I miss you too."

(Ester pauses.)

"Well, I have to get back to loading, seems like we're on duty twenty-four hours a day. The good news for us, Mom, is that I'm coming home soon; they said by Christmas! Until then, I'm holding you both in my heart and my prayers.

Your loving son,

Darnell

(Ester folds the letter and places it back in the satchel. Ester and Loretta embrace as Pastor Franklin enters the scene)

PASTOR FRANKLIN

Ms. Williams, Loretta, it's time for our service; please follow me.

(Ester and Loretta sob quietly and follow the pastor. Lights fade from the casket and illuminates the podium side. The honor guards are standing on separate sides of the podium. The pastor is standing at the podium and the military representative is to his left holding triangular folded American flag.Ester clutches the satchel as she and Loretta stand holding on to each other)

MILITARY REPRESENTATIVE

We will now have our closing prayer, presentation of the flag, and the playing of Taps.

(The honor guards and the military representative are stoically saluting; they have white gloves on. Everyone is standing. Ester and Loretta are embracing.)

PASTOR FRANKLIN

(He is standing at the podium and delivers the prayer with a powerful emotion.)

Let us pray.

Heavenly Father,

Today, we are not surrendering Darnell's soul; we are lifting him with the songs of our people who will continue to do your work here on earth.

Lord . . . Ms. Williams shared with me that Darnell came into this world fighting for his life, being premature, but he left this life fighting for others ...and for that sacrifice, we will always feel his presence...(Pause)...so that when we exhale from that deep breath of freedom...we can walk down the street with renewed courage and greet our neighbors without worry or concern and believe in our own hearts the words that gave his life purpose...(His voice begins to rise)...to the Republic for which it stands, one nation under God, indivisible, with liberty and justice for all.

In Your precious name we pray.

Amen.

(The military commander walks in with the folded flag and presents Ester with the flag.)

MILITARY COMMANDER

On behalf of the President of the United States, the United States Navy, and a grateful nation please accept this flag as a symbol of our appreciation for your loved one's honorable and faithful service.

(Ester accepts the flag and nods to the representative as she and Loretta embrace. Loretta glances toward the sky and gasps in astonishment.)

LORETTA

Look, Mom, an eagle!!!

(Ester looks through tears at the sky and gasps and raises her hand toward the sky.)

ESTER

Oh, Loretta . . . look at him . . . soar!

(Ester softly smiles while clutching the flag. Loretta and she hold each other and continue looking at sky. The spotlight slowly goes dark to the playing of Taps.)

THE END

THE PLAYWRIGHT

A writer expresses her frustration in dramatic detail to her husband as she admonishes the limitations that society continues to place on her creative musings.

CHARACTERS

James 30+ - wearing loose faded jeans and a faded Nirvana concert t-shirt. He is a laid-back guy.

Patrice 30+ - dressed in one of James's shirts and pajama shorts; hair is pulled back. She is a passionate playwright.

(They are a married couple.)

STAGE SETTING

A couch, notebooks, pens and a remote for TV on the couch.

Patrice and James are sitting on opposite ends of the couch. James is half asleep and slumped and Patrice is sitting on the edge writing quickly in her notebook. She pauses.

PATRICE

(Patrice speaks enthusiastically.)

Hey, what about this idea, honey? Listen to this idea . . . honey . . . are you *asleep?*

JAMES

(He is startled from his nap and quickly sits up.)

Oh . . . what was that honey? You got an idea?

PATRICE

You're not listening to me! C'mon, I need you to listen and see what you think!

JAMES

Oh, ok.

(He wipes his eyes quickly and now sits halfway slumped.)

PATRICE

Ok, the play is called *There's something about Darling Nikki*. It's based on the story behind Prince's song and the origins of the Parental Advisory sticker. It seems that the song is about masterba—

JAMES

Wha . . . wha . . . whooo . . . wait a minute. C'mon, honey. Isn't that a little too . . . too . . . like not cool to write about?

PATRICE

(Patrice laughs heartily.)

What? That's the point; you gotta make the comfortable *un*comfortable, then bring it back to a conclusion that guides your audience into *feeling* something. Like maybe unlocking an imprisoned thought . . . kinda.

JAMES

People don't go to the theater to think; they go to be entertained.

PATRICE

(Patrice is now on her feet pacing back and forth, holding her notebook. James continues to be in the same position he has been in, very casually slumped.)

You mean you think controversy or taboo topics aren't entertaining? *God*, it's the epitome of entertainment! Well . . . ok . . . how about this one? I got another one.

There are two middle-aged women arguing about outdated idioms . . . oh no, not that one yet . . . ok, in a small town, there is a ribbon cutting for the new post office, and on the way, the mayor gets a flat tire . . . a . . . a . . . and . . .

(She stutters because she's trying to come up with the next line.)

JAMES

A ribbon cutting . . . boooooring!

(James rolls his eyes.)

PATRICE

BORING? You haven't even heard the story yet. You're not *listening*.

JAMES

You always say that . . . I'm listening, but what I'm hearing does not make sense, and besides I can't always follow that crazy playwright mind of yours.

PATRICE

(She is speaking passionately and lets out a sarcastic laugh.)

Crazy huh? Well, back in the 1950's there was a movement called The Theater of the Absurd. These writers penned such groundbreaking prose . . . like . . . a look at forced conformity, inescapable mantras, a mind-controlling pinball machine, choices between being your real self or falling victim to deception for the sake of having human interaction. (She pauses) Honey! I think it is a play *about a society* that is teetering on the cliff of iconoclasm! Oh God! That's it! (Holding up her pen) I'll write a play about that!

(She sighs.)

JAMES

I think I prefer the ribbon cutting.

(He says impassively.)

PATRICE

(She has now quieted down and appears reflective.)

Gosh, honey. Who am I writing for? Them? The audience? My authentic self? Why can't I be free from these restraints that I have placed in front of me? Am I afraid to offend, provoke? No . . . I'm just reaching for a dialogue that addresses events of both past and present . . . where people from all walks of life can come together and be moved to something. A place where art comes alive. You know the old saying? Art imitates life. I think it's more like *life is imitating art*. Anyway, I'm finding it very hard to write the world's travails in ten minutes.

(She seems dejected now.)

JAMES

I think I prefer the ribbon-cutting scenario.

PATRICE

Honey, I've tried to write about love in the traditional sense . . . but that's over my head . . . give me melancholy, mournful, and morose prose full of unrequited yearnings . . . or . . . a jilted lover . . . or worse . . . a man who leaves his loving wife of thirty years for a younger woman!

JAMES

Well, I'll give you points for being melodramatic! C'mon, Patrice, you don't give yourself enough credit!

PATRICE

I've decided I want to be like . . . like . . . a first responder!

JAMES

You mean you wanna be a paramedic?

(Patrice laughs.)

PATRICE

Well, sort of, I want to save the audience from yet another boring dialogue of the same old, same old. I'll be sort of like a playwright paramedic. Have you seen the typical audience of any given theater?

JAMES

No, I can't say I have, but if you ask me about NASCAR, I'd be all over that.

PATRICE

(She rolls her eyes and speaks sarcastically.) NASCAR . . . now there's an audience with *true* insight on theater matters.

JAMES

That's right! It's a great theater! In fact, four of the greatest words ever spoken from one of the *three* stages of NASCAR: Gentleman, start your engines! Boogity, boogity, boogity!

PATRICE

(She's looking perturbed.)

Ummm, James . . . by the way that's seven words. . .

JAMES

And did you know that all the world's a speedway?

PATRICE

Anyway, you're the only love I'll ever understand. You can take a serious discussion and make it into a comedy. I'm making a mental note of this conversation for a future play on how couples communicate . . . by going off topic!

JAMES

(He slyly smiles.)

You mean we were on a topic?

PATRICE

Funny . . . reeeeal funny. Well, I did have some news about my next book of plays to tell you.

JAMES

Oh? I bet I know the title. You're going to call it . . . "First responders who finally get a pulse from a dying audience."

PATRICE

Oh boy, you're on a roll . . . no! I now have a collaborator!

JAMES

A collaborator?

PATRICE

Yes! Well, you know how I've told you for a long time I've felt like a ship on a stormy sea?

JAMES

Many times, like today for example.

PATRICE

Like a comma without a sentence, an idea without a concept, an adjective without a noun, and then I serendipitously met Macy, who happens to be a playwright and one thing led to another and . . . wow! I'm her Bernie Taupin and she's Elton John.

JAMES

Yeah, like Montana and Rice.

PATRICE

(She looks at him curiously.) Like what?

JAMES

You know one of the greatest QB-WR duos of all time.

PATRICE

QB-WR, what is that?

JAMES

You know quarterback . . . wide receiver.

PATRICE

Okay, you're feeling me . . . in your own way.

So, thank goodness, she's outrageously outgoing and she's an actress providing valuable insight to the cadences of the lines we write! She also shares the same opinion as I do; there truly is the feeling of disequilibrium in the artistic atmosphere, and we'd like to change that!

JAMES

(He says seductively.)

Hey, why don't you bring your equilibrium self over here? (He pats the couch.) Your favorite episode of *Gunsmoke* is on, the one where Miss Kitty says, (talks in cowboy accent) *"When I can't handle a few little bad boys then I'm gonna close up for good!"*

(He laughs and she joins in the laughter. He pretends to click the remote and suddenly Patrice sits up in full alert.)

PATRICE

What? What's that?

(She begins to read out aloud.)

"This program contains outdated cultural depictions. Viewer discretion is advised."

AHHHHHHHH!

(Patrice puts her hand to her face and falls on her husband's shoulder. His expression never changes. Lights go dark.)

THE END

TIME TO FORGIVE

Otis discovers that forgiveness can heal the deep wounds of yesterday, even in the afterlife.

CHARACTERS

African American male - Otis - age 75+

African American male - Otis Jr. - age 50+

Male - Calvin - age 50+

STAGE SETTING

A bench that seats at least three.

Otis is well dressed and sitting alone. Calvin stumbles in jeans and t-shirt and has an injured leg. He makes it to the bench out of breath and in pain.

CALVIN

Ohhh man! I didn't think I was going to make it. You don't mind if I sit here, do you, old man?

(Otis looks at him for a moment and nods slowly. Calvin gets out his handkerchief and wipes his brow.)

I think that was the longest "four" miles I ever walked. I guess this is the abandoned bus stop the warden said I'd pass on the way to town . . . another five and I should be there . . . ow! Damn railroad tracks, I tripped over one of them . . . ow . . .

(Calvin grabs his leg.)

Hey, you can be the first to congratulate me. I just got outta prison . . . spent 30 long years behind those walls of Hamners Penitentiary. You know the one *four* miles from here?

OTIS

Congratulations. (Otis says stoically.)

CALVIN

Ahhh, c'mon, you can do better than that. (Calvin grimaces and grabs his leg.)

Hey, you got a light?

(Calvin pulls out a homemade cigarette.)

Yeah, my boy Johnny gave me this . . . said it was a parting gift. Humph . . . I tell ya what; I ain't gonna miss nobody from that joint.

OTIS

(Otis is stoic.)

I'm sure they feel likewise, and no, I don't have a light.

(Calvin starts wiping his brow again and puts the cigarette back in his pocket.)

CALVIN

Figures . . . I think this is the hottest damn place on earth.

OTIS

Well, no . . . not as hot as . . .

(Calvin looks at him quizzically and interrupts.)

CALVIN

You know something?

(Calvin is starting to get agitated.)

OTIS

What?

CALVIN

I spent the first half of my miserable life a wanted man and now it looks like I'm going to spend the rest of my miserable life *unwanted*! How about that, old man?

The warden said I had paid my debt to society, but I feel like I still have an open tab!

OTIS

(Otis speaks sarcastically.) Be thankful you *have* an open tab; there are people whose tabs are closed out before they were through.

(Calvin looks at him curiously and groans.)

CALVIN

I'll never get a job, I don't have a home, my family won't talk to me . . . nothing! I didn't mean to kill that man! I didn't mean to! I don't know what I was thinking!

OTIS

You weren't.

CALVIN

Just my luck they got a new judge . . . talking about everybody gets equal treatment from the law . . . next thing I know, I get thirty years. I didn't even know that guy . . . it was dark. I panicked and ran after I . . . I . . .

OTIS

Plunged a knife into his heart??

(Calvin grimaces, grabs his leg, and looks at Otis.)

CALVIN

What are you talking about, old man? Either the heat is getting to you, or you done lost your mind.

OTIS

Yes . . . November 10, 1942. It was raining hard that night.

CALVIN

What? (Calvin speaks weakly.)

OTIS

(Otis stoically starts recounting his memory.)

I waited for my son Junior; he had gone to the front of that nightclub to ask for directions; we were lost. After a few minutes, I saw Junior and another man falling from the front door wrestling, struggling.

CALVIN

Wait a minute, old man, how do you know all this? What do you know about anything? That guy came up to my old lady, smiling, whispering in her ear, and I wasn't going to stand for that. I'm a man (Calvin pounds his chest) . . . period.

OTIS

(Otis continues stoically.)

I got out of my car and ran toward the commotion, Junior was getting beat pretty bad. I saw a knife in the man's hand. I threw myself in front of my son just as he moved in and the next thing I knew, I felt a piercing pain in my chest. Everything began to spin . . . the rain in my face, the blurry neon lights of the nightclub, the wide-eyed, shocked faces of bystanders.

CALVIN

How could you possibly know anything about that night? You . . .

OTIS

The last sound I remember hearing were the cries of my son, Junior . . . and you know what? For some strange reason, I had a vision of him when he was just born, crying in his mother's arms. The cries began blending together, then I felt a warmth on that cold ground . . .

CALVIN

Who are you? What are you? I don't have to listen to this . . . I gotta . . .

(Calvin tries to get up and grimaces.)

OTIS

No . . . Calvin.

CALVIN

Hey! How'd you know my name? (Calvin grabbed his leg, trying to deal with who or what Otis is.) Oh God . . . Oh God!

OTIS

(Otis spoke with strong emotion.) I too have been imprisoned . . . imprisoned in an unforgiving heart, and that's why I'm here.

(Otis stands, lifts his shirt, and shows Calvin a wound in his chest. Calvin is open mouthed and shocked.)

I've been existing in purgatory. I was told I needed to learn how to forgive before I could leave there. I never dreamt that something sounding so simple could be so hard but...after thirty years, that wound in my heart has endured its own rehabilitation and...with God's merciful love, I'm almost *healed*. I just have one more thing I gotta . . . *wanna* do . . .

(Otis begins to smile)

. . . and . . . St. Peter is waiting.

CALVIN

You're . . . *Him*!

OTIS

Calvin T. Anderson. . . .. I have come to understand that life is full of wrongdoing, but the inability to forgive, although not covered in the Ten Commandments, is just as sinful. You have taken my life, but you have not taken my soul. I *forgive* you Calvin and I sincerely advise you to clear all your debts before *your* tab is closed for good.

CALVIN

(Calvin speaks humbly.) I'm sorry . . . so sorry. (He drops his head and then looks up.) Is that a start?

OTIS

Goodbye, Calvin . . . there's a chariot waiting for me. I've just gotten out of purgatory, and *you* can be the first one to congratulate *me*!

(Otis smiles and winks at Calvin, who is in a state of disbelief. Otis starts to walk away.)

CALVIN

Hey! Mr. Angel or whatever you are, help me out here. . . .. I can't walk on my own . . . hey! Come back!

(Otis turns around.)

OTIS

Oh, somebody will be along I'm sure . . .

(Otis leaves and starts happily singing "Swing Low, Sweet Chariot" and disappears. Calvin continues to hold his leg.)

CALVIN

Damn heat. Was that a hallucination?

(After a few minutes, a man comes jogging by with sweats on, sneakers, and a white tank top and is breathing hard.)

OTIS JR.

Hey, man! You need some help?

CALVIN

Yes, I hurt my leg! What are you doing in the middle of nowhere?

OTIS JR.

Yeah, right? Just so happens I'm a coach at an after-school program downtown. I gotta try and stay in shape; those kids run circles around me! I usually do this course once a month, good thing it was today, hardly anyone passes through this area.

CALVIN

(Calvin says wistfully.)

Yeah . . . except maybe ghosts from the past.

OTIS JR.

(He looks at Calvin curiously.)

Here, let me help you; there's a doctor's office downtown. Wrap your arm around my shoulder.

(The pair get up and start walking clumsily.)

What's your name?

CALVIN

Calvin. What's yours?

(Calvin and Otis Jr.'s voices begin to fade.)

OTIS JR.

Otis, but my friends call me Junior.

CALVIN

(Calvin stops walking and looks at Otis Jr. in disbelief then cries out)

YOU'RE HIM!!

Lights black out.

THE END

RECYCLED SOULS

A new destiny awaits a group of wandering souls as they settle in to meet with their soul assigner.

CHARACTERS

White male - Donnie - age 17+

Black male - Donnie 2 - age 17+

Male (larger-than-life personality) - Cedric - age 40+

Male - Barron - age 50+

Female - Darla - age 20+

SETTINGS

One three-panel partition (Donnie 2 will be hiding behind the partition dressed in hippie clothes and has an electric guitar; he stays hidden from audience until he makes his appearance. One gladiator costume for Barron.)

Three chairs

Three hospital gowns

Three actors are wearing hospital gowns and sitting on the chairs. Donnie is on the far right, next to him Darla, and lastly Cedric, who is wearing neon green eyewear, socks, and crocs.

BARRON

(Barron speaks in a deep, authoritative tone.)

Ok, you restless souls, listen up. Before we begin, has everyone signed their waivers?

(Everyone nods, except Darla.)

DARLA

(Darla raises her hand.)

No, I didn't; this wasn't my intended stop.

(Barron looks perplexed.)

BARRON

Please explain.

DARLA

Well, I began my pilgrimage in earnest but became weary, so I decided to rest on the nearest cloud . . . and just as I was getting comfortable, a voice shouted, "Hey you, get off my cloud!" I was startled by the voice and fell through a soft spot. Somehow, I got caught in a windy vortex that led me . . . here.

BARRON

Hmmmmm . . . I see; anything else?

DARLA

Yes, as I was blowing through the entryway, I noticed the word recycle. After reading that, I knew I was in the wrong place . . . because my soul is nonrecyclable.

BARRON

Oh, I'm sorry, Darla, for your turbulent travel, and your commentary is quite notable but let me clarify, this is a center for those who have decided for themselves that they *wish* and believe that they want to begin again. When it's your time to visit with the soul assigners, please explain your situation to them.

(Darla nods.)

Ok, for the souls who will go on, due to unforeseen circumstances such as your most recent past life's transgression and unkempt karma, we can't guarantee that you won't end up being an invasive species. Any other questions before we begin?

CEDRIC

Will there be any refreshments on the way to our issued birth canal? Nine months is a long time to go without a Chardonnay.

BARRON

Cedric, is that really you? You asked that *same* question in your last cycle!

(Barron laughs.)

Besides, who's to say that you won't end up being a platypus frog; I did glance at your last two hundred transgressions.

CEDRIC

(Cedric sighs.)

Oh my, this is going to be a long afternoon. Oh . . . I do want to mention that I didn't complete my form in section C22. It was the question that required me to check the box that best describes what my soul's preference is, well . . .

(Cedric pauses, then talks quickly.)

I'm not a lost, brave, sensitive, rational, gypsy, kind, or old soul; none of those . . . fit.

BARRON

Did you look on the back page? It mentioned that we are always trying to update our definitions of the wide variety of spirits that levitate in. Cedric, the collective soul matters, so please, let's get together and discuss the newest interpretations later, Ok?

CEDRIC

Awwwww, Barron . . . I love it when you speak French!

(Barron shakes his head in amusement.)

BARRON

Ok! The process goes like this, behind this partition is your soul assigner. After deciding on your next cycle, you will come out and walk past your soul mates one last time and begin your journey as your new self before infancy. Donnie, you're first on the list. I'll be back in a moment; I want to make sure the soul assigner is ready.

(Barron leaves.)

DONNIE

(Donnie pauses, then turns to Darla and Cedric and speaks contemplatively.)

I've decided this time around, I would like an abundance of brilliance dusted along the edges of my soul. I want to really *feel* its complex subtleties so that those conspicuous pieces held captive by unseen forces will burst out and be released through my heart and then through my hands, creating a lavender mist that gently saturates those who take time to understand.

(Cedric and Darla are open mouthed and speechless.)

CEDRIC

Donnie, if anybody can work that out, *you* can. I bet you'll be able to do all that upside down *and* with electrifying magic! We believe in you!!!

DONNIE

Aww, Cedric, you're always looking out for my spiritedness!

BARRON

Ok, Donnie, the assigners are ready.

(Donnie and Barron walk together behind partition.)

CEDRIC

Oh, Darla, this is the exciting part!

(Darla has grown melancholy.)

What's wrong, Darla?

DARLA

Cedric, I'm feeling a little depleted. Do you think the soul assigner will be able to help me?

CEDRIC

Yeeeeess! I'm sure they can . . . I bet your karma is as clean as a whistle and you seem to be the sort to have minimum transgressions. Here, rest your head on my shoulder . . . sometimes star-trekking can be tiresome and cloud-dodging too! Once, when I hadn't fully transitioned, I was ascending and BAM!

(Cedric slaps the one side of his head.)

I hit my head on an iCloud, and it nearly knocked me out!

(Cedric rattles off quickly.)

I had visions of apples, calendars, ringtones, apps, third-party accessories, and cryptic encryptions for days!

(Darla seems tired but listens amusingly and yawns.)

DARLA

Cedric . . . where I'm going, it's not karma or transgressions that are noted but other things.

CEDRIC

Oh? Like what?

DARLA

Well, believing in—

BARRON

Ok, hereeees, Donnie!!

(Donnie2 struts in holding a guitar and smiling, wearing hippie clothes)

DONNIE2

Hey soul mates, check this out!

(Donnie holds up the guitar.)

The assigners said that this will help me change the world but I'm not sure how . . . but hey, let me give you a sample. I have a band of experienced angels that will help me out . . . ready?

(Darla, Cedric, and Barron nod with excitement.)

(Donnie2 holds the guitar and emulates playing with enthusiasm for about 14 seconds as the theatre speakers pipe in electric guitar music that is available on public domain)

(Darla, Barron, and Cedric clap enthusiastically.)

DONNIE2

Pretty right on . . . right?

CEDRIC

Amazingly electric!!!

DONNIE2

Well... it's time for me to absorb moonbeams and fly with the other soaring souls. Goodbye friends, it's time to go... I hear my cloud train a comin'.

... to take me far... from this pivotal place... (He saunters offstage)

CEDRIC

Bye! Or will it be . . . hi?

(Cedric laughs and waves, but Darla is becoming more tired.)

BARRON

Ok, Darla, I'll be right back; you'll be next.

(Darla has now slumped down in the chair.)

CEDRIC

Darla! Hang on! Don't let your spirit rest until it's secured! A lazy soul can be easily distracted and become . . . lost!

DARLA

I don't know about that. I just want to get to my home . . . to the city of angels . . . where the streets are—

CEDRIC

You mean you're going to Los Angeles? Oh my gosh, you really did get blown off course!

DARLA

(Darla laughs wearily.)

No . . . not exactly. . . . Oh, Cedric, you certainly are a one-of-kind soul; maybe you should put *that* on the C22 form.

CEDRIC

Darla, I'm pulling out all the stops watch because I have a dance for you.

(Cedric gets up and turns around twice and mimics a brief soft shoe tap dance and stops and looks at her.)

That was my good luck happy dance . . . for you.

DARLA

Are you sure it wasn't because you had an itch that you couldn't reach?

CEDRIC

Funny, Darla, very funny. Ok, oh yes! I remember a story ... it was about three lifetimes ago, to make it home, this young girl was instructed to click her heels three times like this.(He clicks his heels and almost trips) Well, it worked for her maybe ...

(Barron appears.)

BARRON

Darla, let me help you; it's time . . .

(Barron escorts Darla behind the partition. Cedric is sitting down crossing his fingers; after a few moments Barron appears with a serious look.)

CEDRIC

What happened to Darla?

BARRON

(Barron pauses before speaking, then takes a deep breath and releases.)

The one who presides over this realm personally came to her aid. I watched them ascend together wrapped in a honey-colored light . . . and then they paused momentarily. Darla looked over her shoulders. She said, "Be sure to tell Cedric his dance worked and that I'll never forget the one-of-a-kind soul who wears crocs and neon-colored glasses." And then they disappeared into an iridescent sky.

CEDRIC

(Cedric dabs at his eyes and smiles.)

Oh, I just love happy beginnings!

BARRON

Yes, thank goodness! Hey, Cedric, let me take you to somewhere special; there's this new place just past Cirrus Circle called the Soul Kitchen run by some guy named Jim, I hear it's got great spiritual energy and poetry reading. What do you say?

(Barron extends his arm.)

CEDRIC

Yeah . . . it's about time I redeemed that rain check you gave me 89 lifetimes ago!

(Barron and Cedric walk out arm in arm laughing.)

Lights go dark.

THE END

THE AUDITION

A young woman attempts to land a part in a play.

CHARACTERS

African American Woman - Ms. Simpson 50+

Light-skinned Biracial Woman - Teesa Andrews 20+

Male - Security guard 50+

African American male - Mr. Franklin 60+

STAGE SETTING

2 chairs and a desk with 2 stacks of papers, an old lamp and an array of pencils.

Teresa is wearing thin rimmed glasses like Rosa Parks and wears 50's style clothing.

Ms. Simpson sits at the table writing her notes and hears someone enter the door and raises her eyes just enough to acknowledge the woman who has entered.

MS. SIMPSON

Yes? What can I do for you? Are you here for the audition?

TEESA

(She speaks with self-assurance.)

Yes, I'm here to audition for the Rosa Parks play, are you Ms. Simpson?

MS. SIMPSON

(Ms. Simpson speaks in an authoritative tone.)

Yes, I'm Ms. Simpson, but you must have the wrong date; today is for Rosa Parks auditions only. The extras for the bus scene will be Thursday. You'll find the schedule posted outside the door on the wall adjacent to the water cooler.

TEESA

Ms. Simpson, I *want* to audition for the part of Rosa Parks. (She speaks proudly.) I've studied her extensively and feel quite confident I can be the Rosa Parks your theater company would be proud of and . . . I feel honored to have this opportunity.

MS. SIMPSON

(She puts her pencil down and looks at Teesa with a smirk.)

You mean to tell me you are here to audition for the part of *Rosa Parks*?

TEESA

Yes, ma'am.

(Ms. Simpson squirms in her seat momentarily, scratches her head and adjusts her eyeglasses, and reaches out for Teesa's resume.)

MS. SIMPSON

Well, Ms. Andrews, I'm not seeing anything here on your resume that qualifies you for our production. Yes, I see you've performed with the National Historic Figures Acting Troupe, and you've won several awards for your portrayal of Martha Washington but . . . this . . . is . . . different. You are not right for an accurate portrayal of Rosa Parks.

TEESA

Well, yes, it is different, Martha Washington is no Rosa Parks and vice versa . . . but accurately? I'm confused at that . . .

MS. SIMPSON

(She is clearly rattled.)

What? I *said* you are not right for this part.

TEESA

Ms. Simpson, this audition was touted as an open audition, so I felt that my inexperience wouldn't be a problem. Please . . . could you just give me a chance? I have prepared my monologue and . . .

MS. SIMPSON

NO! As I said, you are not *right* for this part; look, why don't you come back Thursday, ok?

TEESA

(Teesa sits up straight and speaks calmly but with a terse tone.)

Ms. Simpson, is it ... because of my *color* ... (she touches her arm) or lack of? Let's just cut to the chase. (She is now speaking angrily.) I can read you like a worn-out script! I'm sure you know Ms. Parks was multiracial and so (speaking sarcastically) was hoping that you might have a shred of integrity behind your facade! Please, we *all* have come a long way.

MS. SIMPSON

(She slams her pencil down.)

Ms. Andrews *please!* I know all I need to know about Rosa Parks without a lecture. As I stated, you are not right for the part, *good day!*

TEESA

(She feigns despair.) Why do I suddenly feel like I'm being confronted by James Blake himself? You know (speaks sarcastically) the bus driver who was on duty that fateful day when Ms. Parks had had enough! Wow! (Speaks mockingly) Ms. Simpson, maybe *you* should audition for James Blake!

(They both stand up the same time, both are angry, both are staring each other down.)

MS. SIMPSON

(A sarcastic smile grows on her face, then she speaks angrily.)

Well, I never ...! Ms. Andrews ... GET OUT! (She gestures toward the door.)

TEESA

(Teesa is still standing.)

What are you going to do, call Montgomery Police Officer Leroy Pierce? You know the guy, the officer who first responded to a call about a bus driver having problems with a black woman because of where she was sitting! (She starts raising her voice angrily.) You see, Ms. Simpson, I know my history! I know the story! I *know* her life, I was born to play this part! (She flops down in her seat and holds on to the edges.)

I'm not getting up. (She said matter-of-factly.)

MS. SIMPSON

SECURITY! SECURITY!

(A security guard runs in.)

SECURITY GUARD

What is it, Ms. Simpson??? (He is on full alert, looking around trying to see the perpetrator. Teesa is sitting in the chair, nonchalantly smiling.)

MS. SIMPSON

Remove her from the chair! She's . . .

SECURITY GUARD

Then what?

MS. SIMPSON

She's refusing to get out of her seat! I told her to leave! Get her out!

SECURITY

Uncooperative? This is a first. Ok, Ms. Simpson. (He turns to Teesa.) Miss, you'll have to go.

TEESA

Oh, I'm not getting up. (She states matter-of-factly.)

SECURITY

Miss, you have to get up and leave.

TEESA

Not happening.

SECURITY

(The guard speaks regretfully.) Please, don't make me get physical.

TEESA

I'm not making you do anything.

SECURITY

Ok, you leave me no choice!

(The security guard takes the back of Teesa's chair and starts to drag it. Teesa grabs the table and the seat, and the table begins to move.)

MS. SIMPSON

LET GO OF THAT TABLE!

(Teesa digs in and holds on while the security guard inches Teesa, the chair, and the table closer to the door when suddenly . . .)

MR. FRANKLIN

(A well-dressed man rushes in.)

WHAT IS GOING ON HERE?

(Everyone immediately freezes.)

MS. SIMPSON

Oh, Mr. Franklin! I'm so sorry for this outburst; we are having a small problem.

MR. FRANKLIN

Problem? It sounds like a 1950's protest! I thought . . . wait a minute, our play doesn't begin for another two months! (He kind of laughs as if to shrug off the commotion.)

MR. FRANKLIN

(He looks slightly confused at the situation)

Ms. Simpson, what is going on?

(Everyone starts talking at once.)

SECURITY GUARD

Well, I ran in here thinking I was . . .

MS. SIMPSON

She wouldn't leave when I asked her . . . she . . .

TEESA

That lady (she points at Ms. Simpson) was not giving me the chance . . .

MR. FRANKLIN

STOP!!!!! Well, Ms. Simpson, I knew you were innovative, but this surpasses any expectations I had of you as our casting director!

MS. SIMPSON

What . . . ?

MR. FRANKLIN

Now I get it; you were staging some sort of reenactment! And by the looks of it, this actress Miss . . . Miss . . .

TEESA

(She has a surprised look on her face and continues to hold on to her seat.)

Teesa Andrews.

MR. FRANKLIN

Well, Ms. Andrews, as the director of this production, let me be the first to congratulate you on getting the role of Rosa Parks! It's quite apparent to me that you have what it takes, and I commend you (he looks at Ms. Simpson) for seeing the talent in Ms. Andrews. Just look at how she continues to grip her seat. I can only imagine that must have been an emotion Rosa Parks felt in her heart . . . the importance of holding on . . .

MS. SIMPSON

(She is looking wide-eyed.)

Umm . . . Mr. Franklin . . . it really didn't—

TEESA

(Teesa talks loudly and happily.)

Oh, thank you, Mr. Franklin! *Yes* . . . it was an avant-garde approach. (She glances over at Ms. Simpson and narrows her eyes quickly, then changes her expression and looks back toward Mr. Franklin.) But that's why I value your theater group; its stellar reputation for presenting programs that not only teach but also touch the hearts of all those who attend in a creative, *provocative* way, dispelling preconceived notions toward prejudices both known and unknown. (She glances over at Ms. Simpson smugly.)

MR. FRANKLIN

(He looks toward the security guard.) You can leave now, but thank you very much for your quick response . . . to this lady who refused to get out of her chair. (He slightly smiles).

SECURITY

Yes, sir. (He exits the stage.)

MR. FRANKLIN

Ok, I'll have to get back to my work combing through some details . . . lighting issues, staging, and all those eceteras but I'm relieved our main portrayal of a remarkably iconic woman has been cast. (He exits stage.)

MS. SIMPSON

Why did you do that?

TEESA

Do what? (Teesa gets up and smoothes her clothes out and looks at Ms. Simpson.)

MS. SIMPSON

Not tell him the truth.

TEESA

Well . . . truth can be subjective, but I will say this; my mother always told me to listen to the songs in my soul and I heard one today and it sang of forgiveness.

(Ms. Simpson is speechless and sits down and takes off her glasses.)

MS. SIMPSON

Ms. Andrews, please report to the theater auditorium at 2:00 p.m.; you'll be meeting other actors and we'll begin the process of sorting through our dialogue direction.

TEESA

Ok, thank you; I'll show myself to the door.

(Lights go down on Ms. Simpson and come up on the far left of stage where Teesa enters and dials her phone.)

Mom? (She pauses.)

You are talking to the newly cast, Rosa Parks! (She pauses again.)

Yes!

Oh, you're just outside? I'm on my way! (She does a fist pump.)

Lights go dark.

THE END

TWO TICKETS

A knock on the door thwarts a woman at the end of her rope from making a bad decision.

CHARACTERS

Female - Jenna age 50 +

Female – Carmen age 50+

STAGE SETTING

There is a dining room table with dirty dishes, silverware, a knife and several stacked pieces of paper/bills.

One couch is needed and a lamp that stands next to it. There is one hippie styled vest hidden offstage for Jenna to retrieve later in the play.

The lighting is dim and dingy. A tapping of a cane can be heard, in walks Jenna, a 50 something woman who is in despair.

JENNA

(Jenna approaches the table with great difficulty and slams her cane on the table)

This is bull! I can't even keep a clean house. (She bends and rubs her aching knee)

I don't want another knee replacement; I just want to be well damn it! My heart is broken and so is my good for nothing body. Why do I even try?

(She grabs loose paper on the table and angrily throws them on the floor)

Bills, bills, bills! (She starts to weep.) I can't pay them!

(She spots a knife on the table. She continues to sob, first softly, then it gets more audible)

I can't . . . (She stutters.) I . . . can't anymore . . .

(Jenna takes the knife in her hand and slowly sinks to the floor with her back to the couch. Her eyes look around the room.)

It's so . . . lonely.

(She says softly with a lingering, painful sob. She looks at the knife and sees her reflection and blinks and begins to softly cry).

I used to be so happy. What happened? How did I get here? He always said I had pretty eyes.

(She wipes a tear and places the knife along her wrist.)

Well, just a bunch of lies! Lies! Lies!

(Her voice rises with each syllable and then silence. Jenna is now closing her eyes and begins to realize that she is going to cut her wrist. She grimaces and just at that moment, there is a loud pounding on the door.)

CARMEN

Hey girl! Let me in! I know you're home. I just saw your cat run past the lanai and you never leave Pookie out!

(She laughs heartily.)

(A shocked Jenna swallows hard and struggles with deciding on whether to harm herself or answer her friend)

C'mon! (Pound! pound!) Open the door! I have a surprise for you!

(Carmen finds the hidden key, unlocks the door, and enters slowly. Jenna hides the knife under the sofa)

Hello! Jenna? What are you doing on the floor? Are you ok?

JENNA

Ahhh . . . yes, I'm just cleaning these baseboards!

CARMEN

(Heartily laughing as she places the key on the table.)

Yeah sure! All the years I've known you I ain't never seen you bother with that! I know! Really you probably dropped the last chocolate chip cookie in the house on the floor and you're hoping there really is something to that three-second rule. Never mind! Get up and let me tell you about the craziest surprise I scored today!

(A shocked Jenna wipes her eyes and stands up, sits on the sofa and faces Carmen, who is standing with her hands behind her back.)

JENNA

Carmen, this just isn't a good time . . . I . . .

CARMEN

(Carmen laughs and walks over to the couch and sits by Jenna) Oh, I know; you'll change your tune when I tell you what's in my back pocket!

JENNA

(Jenna sighs.) Unless it's a bazillion dollars, I'm not interested.

CARMEN

(Carmen laughs.)

Oh, it's waaaaay better!

JENNA

Carmen, I'm not up for company. I don't mean to sound rude but . . .

CARMEN

Rude? Nah . . . I can see you were in the middle of one big pity party; it appears you have just won pin the tale on the loser! Look at you! Your eyes are as red as that time we stayed up all night after the Sly and the Family Stone concert, and Sly has nothing to do with this; you're not fooling me for one minute. (Carmen says sarcastically.) Oh wait . . . I know . . . Carl.

JENNA

Well . . .

CARMEN

Aww . . . c'mon, Jenna! This is getting ridiculous; how many years are you going to invest in a lousy lot? There's nothing but weeds and an overgrowth of empty promises!

JENNA

Well, I guess you could call me a lousy landscaper then, right?

CARMEN

No! It's just . . . you don't love responsibly!

JENNA

What?

CARMEN

You know . . . haven't you heard the info messages in alcohol commercials?

JENNA

Are you comparing love to alcohol now?

CARMEN

(She laughs.) No! I'm just saying that you always seem to drink down love like there's no tomorrow! Why can't you just sip or ... savor your relationships for once ... responsibly.

Love is one of the strongest elixirs with one of the ... (She smiles) ... sweetest hangovers ... but Jenna ... you always go back to the hair of the dog that bit you!!

JENNA

No, I don't!

CARMEN

And another thing ... I bet you watch that "happy ending" romance channel ... right?

JENNA

Well, sometimes. When I watch those movies, I know what I'm going to get, so your analogies or metaphors or whatever are losing here.

CARMEN

Well, when you watch one of those movies you know what you're in for. There's always the typical happy ending but, Jenna, that's in the movies and what's going on with you is no movie. . . . . You skipped the auditioning part and . . . you've already written your end before the story can play out. Hey, those sappy stations you watch know the screenplay you want...that's why you turn it on...to escape and pretend... then sadly you apply their ending to your beginning!

JENNA

Oh God . . . here you go; I'm seventeen all over again!

CARMEN

Aha! Guilty as charge . . . you just confessed! The plot thickens, our protagonist has now inadvertently fessed up! I love these twists! See? You yourself revealed that your approach to love hasn't budged . . . and here we are.

JENNA

The only thing twisted is your mind! (Jenna laughs.)

Ok . . . ok! I get what you're saying.

CARMEN

The other thing . . . would you hand over your life's savings to just anyone?

JENNA

Of course not!

CARMEN

No, you wouldn't! Then why hand someone the most valuable thing that is yours and yours alone, the one thing that keeps you alive with possibilities!

JENNA

But Carl . . . he's always doing—

CARMEN

Jenna, did you know the word *blame* has the word *me* in it? Blame is easy to throw around when things are tough, but it really means you must take responsibility . . . *with your love*! The blame game is always a part of deception's tactics; stop allowing it to enter your space.

JENNA

Hmmm.

CARMEN

Be kind to yourself, Jenna. I'm always kind to myself and you know what?

JENNA

Oh God, there's more lecturing?

CARMEN

(Carmen laughs.) No . . . I got so much kind going on, I'm going to share it with you! After all, you and I have been down so many rocky roads together but . . . tonight, guess what?

JENNA

(Jenna speaks cautiously.) What?

CARMEN

(Carmen yells enthusiastically.)

I scored two tickets to KC and the SUNSHINE BAND tonight only!

(Carmen begins to dance around.)

Remember your favorite song "I'm Your Boogie Man?"

JENNA

We used to boogie to that band all night long. (She says reminiscing.)

CARMEN

The catch is we got to go. Well, like now! We can get take-out at your favorite Chinese restaurant and tailgate in the Casino parking lot! Now I know you're not going to say no. . . . This is just like old times again! Remember when we got backstage in '75 at that old arena! (Carmen laughs.) You wore those tight faded bell-bottoms with a crop top, and I had my favorite midi skirt and knee-high boots with a crochet halter! We had those roadies eating from our cheese doodle fingers!

(Jenna is now more relaxed but still has an expression that doesn't go unnoticed by Carmen.)

CARMEN

Jenna, are you cool now?

JENNA

(Jenna speaks cautiously.) I'm . . . I'm good.

(Her voice starts to rise in enthusiasm.)

KC, wow this is ... just crazy! I've got to change really quick .... ok?

CARMEN

Ok, I'll wait in the car. I'm parked by the mailboxes to the right of your apartment.

(Carmen exits the stage dancing and humming as Jenna briefly walks off the other side of the stage. Jenna quickly re-emerges wearing a hippie-styled vest walking with her cane while looking over at the chaos on the floor.)

JENNA

(Jenna sighs heavily.)

Wow, what the heck was I thinking?

(She calls out to her pet cat.)

Pookie! Mama's leaving, be a good little kitty, okay?

(She looks around for a minute.)

Looks like I have some cleaning up to do . . . tomorrow.

(She smiles)

I'm grateful for who I am; I'm just going to have to accept that I'm not 24 anymore. But I still fit pretty good in my jeans, and besides, I NEVER dance responsibly. I'm one helluva pole dancer! (She laughs and hoists her cane in the air then smacks it down on the ground and hears a car horn blow from outside. She smiles and begins to do her dance rendition with her cane seductively. She's humming and shaking her booty and out the door. Lights out.)

THE END

EPITHET REDUX

Two sisters argue over the gravestone inscription of their mother.

CHARACTERS

Female - Sandra - age 50+

Female - Lisa - age 60+

Male - Preacher - age 70+

STAGE SETTING

One gravestone and a large purse for Sandra to carry, that has duct tape, paper and a sharpie inside.

(The two sisters are standing by the gravestone of their recently passed mother).

SANDRA

(Angrily reading the gravestone.)

A hoot? What in the *hell?* I suggested that we put a Mark Nepo quote on Mom's headstone, you know, the one that reads, *"No bird can fly without opening its wings."*

But you had them inscribe that . . . she was a hoot? (She says angrily.) You *know* how she loved birds! All of us do.

(Sandra looks at Lisa.)

What a *disgusting* lie! A *hoot?!* She was far from that!

I have a good mind to punch you like I was going to do when I was fifteen.

LISA

What? Well.... hoot.... isn't that what an owl says? (She laughs sarcastically.) Didn't you just tell me Mom loved birds?

SANDRA

It was a good thing I threw my shoulder out before landing a punch back then, but I *know* it won't pop out now! How *dare* you! (She raises her fist.) You just wanted one last "*screw you*" to Mom.

LISA

Oh, shut up! I spoke with other family members and they all agreed on it.

SANDRA

Agreed on? Huh? I didn't agree on anything! By the others you mean . . . our brothers. They probably just wanted to move on and would have agreed to "here she lies" and that's it.

LISA

Well, you didn't respond to our family social media page.

SANDRA

I don't use social media platforms! Whatever happened to phone calls?

LISA

Well, that's not my problem . . . and by the way, social media is far more productive, but then, *productive*? That sure as hell ain't you.

SANDRA

And another thing, I've been chomping at the bit to lay into you about . . . how could you just put Mom in a pair of jeans and a turtleneck!

LISA

So, what about it? I saw a good deal at the discount store and that outfit was perfect.

SANDRA

Perfect? Perfect for whom?

You put Mom in clothes from a discount store when you knew she wanted to be buried in her dress that reminded her of Monet's Garden?

LISA

(She says sarcastically.) I thought it was a nice gesture.

SANDRA

Well...I one-upped you big sister! Last night after her wake,I took mom's dress to the funeral director knowing we were having a closed casket service and had them change her into what she wanted... (her voice quivers)...now... she can lie in peace in Monet's Garden! So there...how about that!!!

(Lisa gasps.)

SANDRA

You always hated Mom . . . hated her for who she . . . *wasn't*. She wasn't the kind to wipe your sissy tears when you had a boo-boo. (Sandra speaks sarcastically.)

LISA

That's not what—

SANDRA

And she wasn't the kind of mom that went to your parent–teacher conferences. I'll tell you the kind she wasn't she wasn't a *fake*. She never hid the fact that she was a miserable alcoholic. Instead of us smelling pancakes and bacon for breakfast, it was always cigarette smoke and stale beer.

LISA

But you . . .

SANDRA

My clothes never matched because I never could find any clean ones . . . but damn it, I pieced them together. No, Mom wasn't a fake and there's something to be said about that. She never tried to hide who she was.

LISA

Well, you were always causing problems at home. Mom and Dad had to run to school every other week because you were getting suspended; you got kicked off the track team and they tried to get you back on it, but you ran away, then showed up two days later with nothing to say for yourself . . . so disgusting. And let's not forget the time you told Mom you would kill her with your bare hands if she touched any of your *crappy* Southern rock albums!!

You were such a . . . brat.

SANDRA

Well . . . here we are right?

She's gone . . . but . . . (she gestures toward the gravestone) she was a *hoot?* That is the ultimate swipe etched in stone for all eternity . . . so disrespectful. Just forget it . . . you're probably going to go back to your tidy home and escape from your truth and swallow it down with one of your Beaujolais wines and a slice of cheese . . . good for you.

LISA

I don't have to listen to this. I'm leaving.

SANDRA

(Sandra speaks sarcastically.)

Don't forget to take those memories that never *were* . . . with you, ok?

LISA

(Lisa angrily replies.) What do you mean?

SANDRA

You know; you're the one who majored in philosophy. (Sandra speaks sarcastically.)

LISA

Well, I don't.

SANDRA

Well maybe you're not the smart one.

(The preacher enters the stage and walks up to the sisters)

PREACHER

I'm sorry for interrupting and I'm equally sorry that I overheard some of your conversation. I just felt that I needed to intercede and share with you something I have learned over time; may I?

LISA

Fine (She crosses her arm and turns slightly away from him.)

SANDRA

Whatever. (She stands stoically.)

PREACHER

You see the ground here? (He gestures over the grave.) It's all churned up and disturbed because there's a deep wound hollowed out, a place where all the sorrows, joys, and moments of someone's life will be placed, and then sometimes there are tears that fall into that abyss, leaving behind a small part of a loved one's loss and then, soon after, family and friends leave, total strangers begin to refill the darkness with rich fertile soil that has been tilled and turned with care and respect . . . over time, that mound of earth will pack down and seemingly from nowhere, the grass will grow back lush and green once again watered by heavenly tears of joy and healing the once-gaping wound of yesterday.

SANDRA

Thank you, Preacher, for your kind words.

(Preacher nods and walks offstage. Sandra looks at Lisa)

Mom wouldn't want your fake tears, so take them with you too . . . and—

(Lisa interrupts.)

LISA

I guess you weren't listening to a word he said!

SANDRA

No, I wasn't but what I *do* know . . . is that she had a strange kind of love for us, and you could never accept that.

LISA

And I suppose you did?

SANDRA

Yes . . . I did and still do.

LISA

You're impossible!

(Lisa storms off.)

SANDRA

(She reaches into her purse and pulls out paper, pen and duct tape, then kneels down beside the tombstone to write. After writing, she tapes the paper over the inscription and stands).

SANDRA

(Sandra clears her throat and reads aloud.)

Gladys Goodman

August 5, 1934–January 4, 2021

Lived and loved her life her way.

No bird can fly without opening its wings . . .

Now you can fly...free bird.

There . . . fixed it.

(Sandra looks around and then walks away.)

Lights go dark.

THE END

GETTING OUR DISORDER IN ORDER

An illness threatens to sabotage the job Della is hoping for.

CHARACTERS

Female- Della - florist - age 20+

Female- Val - age 20+

STAGE SETTING

One table, a laptop opened, a chair and a beautiful flower arrangement, one couch, and a notebook.

(Della is pacing while wringing her hands. Val walks in.)

VAL

Oh hey, sorry I'm late, it took the groomer and two of his assistants to get Virginia Woof out of her back seat harness. You know, for a miniature Schnauzer, she's pretty strong!

DELLA

Strong willed more like it! Thank God, you're here. I need you to help calm me down; my callback interview for the florist position is in twenty minutes!

VAL

I know, honey.

(She walks up and hugs her.)

You got this! You have been doing so well . . . making these beautiful arrangements, keeping up with your appointments, and eating healthy. I'm really proud of you, Della.

DELLA

(Della is not listening) Oh God!

(Della continues to pace. Val sits down on edge of the couch.)

I feel like a tossed-aside Rubik's cube, forgotten, useless . . . a passing fad that's been cashed out in someone's memory bank.

VAL

Okay . . . now *where* did that come from?

Della! *C'mon*, don't go there! You know where that's going to lead? To nowhere!

(Della is pacing and still is wringing her hands.)

146

DELLA

Oh, listen to what I came up with to pitch to the flower shop! I want to know what you think.

(Della sounds agitated; she clears her throat and stands like a ringmaster in a circus.)

Come one! Come all!

(Della points at Val.)

You too can have my new creation, the bipolar arrangement, (her voice rises and she becomes animated while describing) ... on one side of this floral fantasy you will see the sad side, turn it around to find...yes... that effervescent and elusive happy side!!!

VAL

Della, sit here please. This waxing and waning can cause you to cycle. Did you take your meds?

DELLA

I'm sorry; I guess I'm in my "*mixed mood.*"

(Della says that using air quotation marks with her fingers.)

You know, a real cocktail with just the right amount of agitation, low self-esteem, and a generous amount of self-deprecation garnished with a sprig of grandiosity!

(Val pats the couch. Della grudgingly plops down next to Val.)

VAL

You're pulling your triggers; don't let your disorder be your weapon against yourself. Remember, *use* the shield of your soul and the grit *you* own . . . courageously bold and unwavering in determination to overcome obstacles...both seen and unseen.

DELLA

Oh God, did you read that on one of those *lame* posters at one of the outpatient clinic rooms?

(Della rolls her eyes and snickers.)

What if I don't get the job?

VAL

What if you do?

(Val smiles.)

Look at that; you did that!

(She points to the arrangement on the table.)

That was created by your gentle hands and a loving heart . . . something beautiful that resides in you comes through in your arrangements. Who knew beauty could be so big in a small vase?

DELLA

Now if I could only arrange my brain like I do my flowers!

VAL

Hey cool . . . that can be another coping mechanism! Remember at the meeting our therapist said for us to help each other find coping skills, something we can do together . . . to get our disorder in order!

(Della and Val snicker as Val reaches for notebook on the side table).

VAL

Let's give this a try. Ok . . . close your eyes. (Della closes eyes.)

Now imagine your mind as an arrangement . . . like ikebana. That's what your mind should be like . . . *arranged* . . . in ikebana style, harmonic balance and minimalism . . . now open your eyes and look at me.

(Della opens her eyes and looks at Val.)

Think of what you have *learned* about ikebana and its purpose...be your own mind ikebanist.

DELLA

Hmm, ok, now that you put it that way . . . I get it. But right now, Val, I'm so tired. I've been overly obsessed about getting this job.

(Della lays against her shoulder and begins to tear up.)

VAL

Oh . . . no . . . no . . . no, you have to get up and move around. C'mon, I'll help.

DELLA

Oh, Val, I just want to sit here.

VAL

Della, remember our therapist suggested for us to move around, so let's do that yoga move . . . Ragdoll!

(Della and Val stand with prayer hands and begin to perform the yoga move Ragdoll, bending over, swinging arms back and forth three times, and then pause.)

VAL

Ok . . . doesn't this feel good?

DELLA

Yes, it does.

VAL

Great, now let's bring it back to prayer pose.

Feel better?

DELLA

(Della sits down on couch.)

Kinda. Val, be honest, is that new medication you've been taking really working?

VAL

Uh-huh, I think so, what do *you* think? (Val joins Della on couch.)

DELLA

Yeah . . . you *have* been somewhat more together; you didn't even yell at me when I left the milk out overnight!

(Val and Della laugh.)

You've always been the strong one anyway.

VAL

No, you are strong . . . just in other ways . . . we balance each other, like yin and yang.

DELLA

Oh God, even my relationship has two sides!

(Della and Val both laugh.)

VAL

No, you know what I *mean*!

(Della looks at her watch.)

DELLA

Oh my God, it's about time!

(There is a sound of phone ringing; Val and Della look at each other as Della answers phone. Val now has her fingers crossed still looking at Della. Della takes in deep breath and answers.)

Hello, this is Della Delaney.

(Pause)

Yes, hello, Ms. Martinez.

(Pause)

Oh, ok, no, weekends and holidays won't be a problem.

(Pause)

Yes.

(Della nods while talking, smiling and looking at Val, who is still on edge of couch crossing her fingers.)

(Pause)

Oh! Oh! That's good news! Thank you so much for this opportunity.

(Pause)

Yes, I can be there tomorrow at three to fill out the paperwork. See you then! Bye.

(Della hangs up.)

I GOT THE JOB!

(Val and Della are now standing and they embrace.)

VAL

No, you have a career! Della Delaney's floral creations for any occasion! You'll have your own shop one day! You'll see! Ok, we don't have to pick up Virginia Woof until 4:30. Let's go get one of your favorite acai bowls at Organic Chickpea!

(Val puts her arm out.)

C'mon, Yin!

DELLA

No, I want to be Yang, you be Yin!

VAL

Well, ok, either way we got both sides covered . . . together.

DELLA

Aww, Val.

(Val and Della laugh and exit the stage.)

Lights go dark.

THE END